Great Moments in Auto Racing

Exciting accounts of the great driving
performances of recent years—the exploits
of stock car champion Richard Petty, Indianapolis
champs A. J. Foyt and Parnelli Jones, Grand Prix
winner Jackie Stewart and many others.

Illustrated with photographs

RANDOM HOUSE SPORTS LIBRARY

Great Moments in
Auto Racing

BY FRANK ORR

RANDOM HOUSE · NEW YORK

PHOTOGRAPH CREDITS: Alice Bixler, 12, 46, 49 (left), 101, 130; Peter Borsari-Camera Five, 16–17, 42–43, 49 (right); Central Press from Pictorial Parade, 35; Indianapolis Motor Speedway, front and back endpapers, 21, 24 (left); London Daily Express from Pictorial Parade, 77, 117; Paris Match from Pictorial Parade, 4; United Press International, 2–3, 27, 33, 39, 53, 55, 58, 66–67, 81, 85, 87, 89, 115, 122, 126, 134, 142, 146; Cam Warren, 94; Wide World Photos, 19, 24 (right); 28, 64, 65, 70, 74, 99, 105, 107, 110, 136, 141, 145.
Cover photo by Don Hunter.

Library of Congress Cataloging in Publication Data
Orr, Frank.   Great moments in auto racing.   (Random House sports library, no. 4)

SUMMARY: Tales of dramatic triumphs and failures in such automobile racing events as the Grand Prix, Indianapolis 500, and Le Mans.
1. Automobile racing—History—Juvenile literature.
[1. Automobile racing—History]   I. Title.
GV1029.15.O77 1974   796.7′2   73-18087
ISBN 0-394-82763-5   ISBN 0-394-92763-X (lib. bdg.)

Contents

Introduction

Most historians agree that the first official automobile race was staged in 1895 from Paris to Bordeaux, then back to the French capital over 732 miles of dusty, bumpy roads which were little more than cattle paths.

Emile Levassor, an auto construction pioneer in France, won the race in his two-cylinder Panhard at an average speed of 15 miles per hour. By today's standards, the car was scarcely more than a buggy with an engine replacing a horse as the source of power.

The race was a popular event, and large crowds lined the edges of the road when the cars passed through towns and villages. The snail's speed of the cars permitted eager lads to jog alongside—and keep pace—for short distances.

Almost 80 years have passed since Levassor's triumph. Although he was a man of vision, Levassor had no idea of what he had started. From that humble beginning auto racing developed into one of the world's greatest spectator sports, followed by millions, especially in Europe and North and South America.

Small boys no longer run alongside the cars, however, because the speed of auto racing has increased as fast as its popularity. There is little comparison between Levassor's 15 miles per hour and the qualifying speeds at Indianapolis, for instance. Just to get into the race at Indy, a car and driver must be able to average 200 miles per hour on their qualifying laps.

Wherever the fast cars run, there is drama. The sport's appeal is produced by a variety of factors. First, auto racing is perhaps the most dangerous sporting endeavor a man can undertake. The slightest mistake by a driver can produce a crash which may result in death or serious injury for himself and others.

A driver's error or a brilliant maneuver can alter the pattern of a race with shocking speed. The race cars, which are the product of thousands of hours of work and tens of thousands of dollars, may break down under the tremendous stress of racing by the failure of a part that may be worth only a few dollars. And quick changes in weather—a rain shower or an errant gust of wind—may change the complexion of a race in seconds.

But, more than anything, racing brings man and machine together. The driver and his car must perform almost as a single organism in competition against other driver-auto combinations in the race.

The late Jimmy Clark, one of the finest drivers in

history, summed up racing this way: "It is satisfaction, it is disappointment, it is triumph. It is noise, it is color, it is people. For the driver, each race is a new adventure."

Each auto race includes these features in some degree. To the winners, there is satisfaction and triumph; to the losers, disappointment and heartbreak. But for everyone, there is adventure.

The great moments selected for inclusion here were produced in all forms of racing: the glamorous Grand Prix circuit; the Indianapolis 500, the world's richest and most famous sporting event; the Canadian-American Challenge Cup series for big sports cars; stock car racing on the super-ovals of the southern United States; and endurance racing at Le Mans, France.

Some are stories of supreme driving performances by the great names in auto racing history. Others are tales of failure—shocking, dramatic defeats to men and machines when victory appeared to be certain. There are tales of bravery and perseverance, and accounts of men overcoming great handicaps and serious injuries to win.

Every racing devotee has his own list of the great moments in auto racing and to include them all is impossible. Here are a few of the memorable times in a dramatic sport.

FRANK ORR

1

High Bank Millionaire

The superstars of the National Association for Stock Car Auto Racing (NASCAR) were assembled at the front of the field for the 1971 Dixie 500 at Atlanta International Raceway. In the pole position sat Buddy Baker, the fastest qualifier, in his Dodge. Beside him in the front row for the 500-mile grind was Charlie Glotzbach in a Chevrolet. In the second row were Richard Petty and Pete Hamilton in Plymouths. The Allison brothers, Bobby and Donnie, shared the third row in Mercury cars.

The race was part of the long NASCAR Grand National trail, a series of races which ran from late January to early November. Most Grand National races were staged on tracks in the southern United States, where stock car racing was the number one spectator sport and where race drivers were the top sports heroes. Total prize money for the Grand National races was approximately $4,500,000. More than $500,000 of this would be awarded to the leading drivers at the end of the season. The rest was to be awarded as prize money in individual races.

Because rain threatened on race-day morning, only 25,000 spectators came to the Raceway for the Dixie 500. Yet by race time the sun was shining brightly, and a tingle of anticipation ran through the crowd, for this was no ordinary race.

The target of the fans' attention was Richard Lee Petty, the tall, lean man from Randleman, North Carolina, who was driving the brilliant blue Plymouth, marked with the number 43. The son of Lee Petty, three-time NASCAR champion and the greatest stock car racer in the sport's early days, Richard Petty had been in the front ranks of NASCAR drivers from the time he won the rookie-of-the-year award in 1958.

The younger Petty had already set many NASCAR records. The 1971 Dixie 500 was his 551st Grand National race, and he had won a record 133 events, finishing in the top five in 320 races and in the top ten 385 times. In 1967 he had won 27 of 48 races, including a record ten in a row.

On this hot, humid, August day at Atlanta, Petty could add another milestone to his impressive list. He needed to claim only $2,357 in prize money to become the first stock car driver to win more than $1,000,000. A finish in tenth place or better would put him over the magical figure.

Although Petty was regarded as the best stock car racer in the game, several drivers in the Dixie 500 field

Richard Petty watches some practice runs with car sponsor John Holman.

were eager to dispute that claim. The field was fast, deep in superb drivers behind the wheels of excellent cars.

Buddy Baker, sitting in the pole position, was Petty's partner on the Petty Enterprises team. Baker was also the son of a great driver, the legendary Buck Baker, who had often raced wheel-to-wheel against Lee Petty. Pete Hamilton, the blond hot-shot from New England, was one of the few NASCAR drivers from the northern United States, a tough competitor.

Off the track, Bobby and Donnie Allison were quiet, gentlemanly champs. But behind the wheel they became tigers. Bobby Allison and Richard Petty were leading contenders for NASCAR honors in 1971, which frequently placed them close together on the track. Neither man would give up an inch of asphalt to the other, and they had had several fender-bashing duels at high speeds.

The Dixie 500 field of 40 brightly painted cars moved slowly through the warm-up laps behind the pace car. The drivers watched intently for the green flag from the starter, eager to charge ahead when the race began. In the warm cockpit of his Plymouth, Petty was relaxed and confident. His expert crew included his father Lee, manager of the entire Petty Enterprises operation, his brother Maurice, who built the engines, and his cousin Dale Inman, in charge of the pit crew. The Petty Plymouth had been prepared immaculately. Every part had been checked and re-checked to guarantee that the car could finish the 328 laps around the 1.522 mile track, which had corner banking of 18 degrees.

As the field approached the starter's stand, Petty watched for the green flag. But he was also watching the cars around him to determine their strategy. He wanted to run in only one position—at the front of the pack. But the race was a long one, and there was little point in trying to win it on the first turn when the cars were close together and the slightest mistake could produce a huge pile-up.

The pace car pulled off the track into the pit lane, the field gained speed towards the starting line, and the starter waved the green flag. Immediately, 40 right feet pressed their accelerators against the floor-boards, and the big cars roared into the first turn at speeds above 140 miles per hour.

Buddy Baker put his Dodge into the lead. Petty passed Glotzbach to take second place right behind Baker. Glotzbach, Hamilton and the Allisons followed as the fans eased back in their seats for a long afternoon of racing.

Baker held the lead for the first 25 laps, and then Petty took over for 13 circuits. In the first 60 laps Hamilton and Bobby Allison also moved to the front briefly as the field spread out and the front-runners lapped some of the slower cars. The lead changed often as the leaders began to make their pit stops.

On lap 68, Petty, Baker and Bobby Allison were running close together when they narrowly avoided a serious accident. Just as they were coming up on a Dodge driven by Joe Frasson, the car lost a wheel and Frasson spun in front of the three leaders. But after a moment of danger the race continued.

At the halfway mark—164 laps—Petty had taken

the lead for the fifth time. Now it was a four-car race between Petty, Buddy Baker, Pete Hamilton and Bobby Allison. The lead changed hands on pit stops, and the work of the crews became crucial. Petty's crew operated with its usual crisp efficiency, adding fuel, changing tires, wiping the windshield and supplying a drink to the driver in less than 20 seconds on each of his three stops. (During a 20-second pit stop, the other cars gain a mile or more.)

Baker was the first of the leaders to be stopped by the blistering pace. He was leading the race for the tenth time on lap 231 when the engine in his Dodge blew, spewing its oil on the track. The caution flag went up because of the slippery conditions caused by the oil. The other leaders, Petty, Hamilton and Bobby Allison, were within a few car lengths of each other. Then Hamilton's engine quit, leaving only Petty and Allison to battle it out for the top prize.

When Hamilton dropped out, Petty quickly lengthened his lead over Allison to 8.1 seconds, blasting past the slower cars on the straightaways and weaving through them on the turns. Petty made his final pit stop on lap 288 for fuel and two new tires. The stop allowed Allison to move into a 28.2-second lead.

When Allison pulled into the pit lane for his final stop on lap 297, the spectators were on their feet, watching Allison's pit and Petty's car. Allison's crew added fuel, but he rejected new tires to save time. As he rolled out of the pits, Petty's Plymouth roared past into a slight 2.1-second lead over Allison's Mercury.

Allison gradually reduced that lead, and on lap 306 he pulled even with Petty. The fans cheered wildly as the two great drivers battled each other on every corner and down the straights. Each time Allison challenged and attempted to move past, Petty was able to hold him off. Allison moved into a fender-to-fender position through the corners, only to have Petty use his

slightly superior speed on the straights to regain his edge.

Because no more than a car length ever separated the two cars, the machines frequently touched in a hectic bit of fender-bashing entertainment. On lap 312

Petty (43) bumps Bobby Allison's car in the battle for first place.

the cars collided heavily on turn four, and the drivers fought for control to prevent a spin-out. Smoke belched from the skidding tires and when it cleared, Petty had regained his slim lead.

Allison repeatedly tried to pass Petty during the final ten laps but was unable to gain the edge. Petty made no mistakes that would allow Allison to move ahead. The crowd was cheering loudly when the starter waved the checkered victory flag at Petty. After 500 miles of high-speed racing, his margin over Allison was a scant five feet.

Petty drove slowly around the track and pulled into his pit, where he was greeted by his happy crew. He sat in the car for several minutes, exhausted from the heat and labor of the long race. When he did climb through the window (the doors were welded shut for safety), he took a few whiffs from an oxygen tank before walking to the presentation platform.

Petty accepted the traditional victory kiss from the race queen and received a large silver trophy. His share of the race purse plus his awards for leading 179 laps came to $20,200, raising his career earnings to $1,017,853. The win also added another mark to his list of records. It was Petty's 13th super-speedway triumph, one more than the record he had shared with Fred Lorenzen.

If the winning of $1,000,000 was a big thrill for Petty, he kept his excitement well hidden. He accepted congratulations with his usual modesty, claiming that his crew which built and prepared the car at the Petty Enterprises plant in Level Cross, North Carolina, deserved most of the credit.

"More than anything, winning all that money shows

that we have a super team, the best in stock car racing," Petty said. "I'm just another one of the workers on the team, no more important than anyone else. We all work long hours to succeed in this sport.

"Twelve years ago when I was getting started in racing, I didn't know there was such a thing as a million dollars. That was something you read about other folks having but never dreamed of having it yourself. All I wanted to do was make a living for my family.

"It's really something, isn't it? The first money I ever earned was when I was seven years old, a dollar a day holding stalks of tobacco to be tied and cured at my uncle's farm. Things have changed a little since then."

The million-dollar winner holds up his trophy after the Dixie 500.

2

Four Men with a Mission

The 300,000 spectators in the seats at the Indianapolis Motor Speedway became quiet. Then Speedway president Tony Hulman gave the traditional command, "Gentlemen, start your engines." All at once, 33 huge Indy racers roared to life and moved away for the 1961 Indianapolis 500.

The race marked the 50th anniversary of the 500. And although the world-famous event had produced countless moments of drama on Memorial Day, no race in the past and few in the future would match the excitement the spectators were to view on that warm May day in 1961.

The drama of the race would center around four men who were as different in personality and style as chalk and cheese. They came to Indianapolis to win the richest prize in racing, and before they departed,

As the cars come into the first turn in the 1961 Indy 500, Eddie Sachs (12) leads the pack. Also visible are A. J. Foyt (1) and Parnelli Jones (98).

they would give the crowd indelible memories of the race.

In the pole position as the fastest qualifier was Eddie Sachs, the "clown prince of auto racing," a hearty, fun-loving man who had tried to qualify for the 500 five times before making the field in 1957. Sachs was talkative and controversial, a man who lived only to drive fast cars.

Parnelli Jones was in the middle of the second row, an Indianapolis rookie at 27 years of age. He had clawed his way up through the ranks of racing from dirt-track jalopies of California to a sensational record in sprint cars. Jones was a tough, fast, hungry driver. He'd fought hard to get his foot in the door at Indianapolis, and he didn't plan to waste his chance.

Farther back was Rodger Ward, a canny, polished veteran who had won the 500 in 1959 and finished second in 1960. He drove conservatively and had a high finishing percentage. Often he was running long after the chargers had dropped out.

Finally, there was A. J. Foyt, who was in his fourth 500. He would one day become the greatest all-time American race driver. But at 25 years of age, he had not won at Indy, and his long background in jalopies, stock cars, midget and sprint machinery made him a charger who wanted to run only at the front of the pack.

When the race started, Jim Hurtubise jumped into the lead from the outside of the front row and set a record for the first lap with an average speed of 140 mph. Hurtubise was a top stock car racer and a great favorite with the fans. They cheered him on as he held the lead for 35 laps until a piston burned out in his engine.

Defending champion Jim Rathman inherited first place and held it for a few laps. Then Parnelli Jones demonstrated his ability to charge around a race track by passing Sachs, Ward and Rathman in a single lap to move in front.

Driving a roadster nicknamed "Ol' Calhoun," built by the fabled A. J. Watson, Jones retained the lead for 75 laps. Part of this time he drove one-handed. He had been struck on the forehead and cut by a piece of metal thrown up by the wheel of another car. Parnelli used one hand to wipe the blood off his goggles and the other to control his huge machine. He even had to pick his way through the wreckage of a six-car crash, reacting with lightning speed to avoid a car which spun in front of him.

Just when the crowd was convinced that it was Jones' day and a rookie would win the 500, Jones' engine began to make strange noises. One of the four engine cylinders had quit working, forcing him to reduce his speed. Troy Ruttman, Foyt, Sachs and Ward stormed past him. Then Ruttman's clutch failed, and Foyt took the lead, followed closely by Sachs and Ward. The fans were in a frenzy as the lead changed hands several times.

Near the 160-lap mark of the 200-lap race, the three leaders all made the last of three required pit stops in the race. When they were all at racing speeds again, Ward was in the lead, followed by Foyt and Sachs. But Ward's car finally fell to the stress of the fierce competition. Something broke in the chassis, making the car twitchy in the turns. So Ward had to slow down. Foyt and Sachs sped past him.

Now the race was down to two cars. With 20 laps to go, Foyt had built a lead of eight seconds. He appeared to have the victory locked up, but the Speedway is a place where triumph often is snatched away from a man at the last moment.

His car running perfectly, Foyt rolled down the main straight and glanced towards his pit. A crew member was waving a blackboard which had the words "fuel low" scrawled in chalk.

A serious Parnelli Jones before the race and a dejected Rodger Ward afterward—mechanical trouble put him out of contention.

"I thought to myself, 'What the devil is going on?' "
Foyt said later. " 'There's no way that sign could be
right.' I'd made a pit stop a few laps earlier, and I had
to have enough fuel to finish."

During Foyt's pit stop at 160 laps, the nozzle
delivering fuel to his tank had failed to operate
properly, and the correct amount wasn't put in. When
the crew discovered the faulty nozzle, they calculated
how much fuel Foyt had in the tank. It was questiona-
ble if he'd have enough to finish. The crew debated for
several laps whether to order another pit stop.

Many spectators had seen the sign, and a buzz of
excitement swept through the crowd. The crew gave
Foyt a "keep going" signal for several laps. Then with
ten laps remaining, the sign said "come in" and an
angry, frustrated Foyt roared down the pit lane. The
crew hurriedly poured a small amount of fuel into his
tank—they could only spare ten seconds.

Before Foyt could return to the track, Sachs had
roared past into a 15-second lead. Foyt drove his car
very close to the edge, slowing only slightly going into
the corners and drifting up close to the wall coming
out of them, but there appeared to be no chance of his
catching Sachs.

The excited Sachs didn't slow down. His lifelong
ambition was victory in the Indianapolis 500, and the
lead was his with only eight laps to go. Sachs smiled
and waved to his fans, who cheered loudly.

"I think of Indianapolis every minute of my life,
even when I sleep," Sachs once said. "There is nothing
more I want out of life than to win the 500. If I won it,
I'd go out in the street and tell everyone 'I'm Eddie

Sachs and I just won the Indianapolis 500.' "

In the grandstand, someone told Sachs' wife Nancy to go to Victory Lane to meet her husband but she refused to move. Tears ran down her cheeks as she counted down the laps.

Midway through lap 195, Eddie Sachs felt a small bump in the rear end of the car. He glanced back, and his eye caught a flash of white. The rubber was peeling off the right rear tire, and the white liner layer was exposed. His crew saw it, too, and the movement in the pits was seen by the track public address announcer. "Something could be wrong with Sachs' car," he shouted, and the spectators were on their feet immediately.

In his car, Sachs had to make the biggest decision of his life. If he pitted for a new tire, he was certain to lose the race. If he continued to race, there was a chance he would finish and hold his lead. But the tire could also blow out, sending him crashing into a wall. He decided to stop.

"When I saw the white of the tire, I figured the next thing I was going to see was the wall coming at me," Sachs said later. "Well, I'd sooner finish second than be dead."

Three laps remained in the 500 when Sachs pulled into the pit lane and skidded to a halt in his pit. The crew swiftly pulled off the bad tire and installed a new one. When Sachs roared away, a mechanic threw a hammer at his car in anger and frustration.

Just as Sachs reached the end of the pit lane, Foyt sped past into the lead. Sachs drove as hard as he could but was unable to reduce Foyt's lead. At the finish Foyt was 8.28 seconds in front of him.

Foyt's car ran out of fuel soon after he crossed the finish line and took the checkered flag. He had to coast around to Victory Lane. Sachs pulled into the pits and sat in the car for several minutes as if in a state of shock.

Sachs' pit stop and tire change were debated for many months. Some racing people felt that his charging at top speed to widen his lead when Foyt was in the

A. J. Foyt accepts congratulations in the winner's circle.

Eddie Sachs, who lost the race because of a bad tire.

pits had placed strain on the car and tires. Some
believed he should have tried to finish the race on the
bad tire. But tire company technicians who examined
the tire claimed it would have blown had Sachs tried
to run another lap.

Al Dean, who owned Sachs' car, perhaps summed up the situation best when he said, "I wanted him to go on, but then I wasn't driving the car. Who can say what they would have done in Eddie's spot? If the tire had blown and Eddie was killed, I would have felt a lot worse than I did when we lost the race."

Of the four leading drivers in the 1961 Indy race, three went on to abundant success. A. J. Foyt won the race twice more and became the greatest driver in U.S. Auto Club history, a millionaire through investment of his race earnings. Rodger Ward won the 500 for the second time in 1962 and retired in 1967 after an excellent career. Parnelli Jones won at Indy in 1963 and became a legendary racing figure.

But Eddie Sachs' dream of an Indianapolis 500 victory never was realized. He finished third in 1962 and dropped out after 181 laps in 1963. Then in 1964 he died in a flaming crash on the first lap of the Indy race.

Racing is a cruel sport to many of its participants, including Eddie Sachs. Many years after his tragic death, racing fans still wonder: if Sachs had gambled on that worn tire in 1961, would he have achieved his life's ambition—or would he just have died a few years sooner?

3

The King from Brazil

While the majority of auto racing fans in the United States follow home-grown stock and Indianapolis-type races most closely, the only truly international racing is offered by the Grand Prix circuit. In Grand Prix racing, a group of drivers from many countries travels from country to country, participating in a series of races on irregular road courses. The driver who compiles the most points on this circuit of races every year is declared world driving champion.

The Formula 1 cars used for Grand Prix events must meet the stringent specifications (or formula) of the international racing body that supervises the races. They are lighter than Indianapolis cars and must be more versatile. While Indy and stock cars usually race on oval tracks (and therefore face only a long series of left-hand turns), the Grand Prix car must be able to

30

turn sharply in either direction at high speeds and must be able to accelerate and decelerate rapidly to negotiate the irregular Grand Prix tracks.

Two of the regularly scheduled Grand Prix events are run in North America—the U.S. Grand Prix at Watkins Glen, New York, and the Canadian Grand Prix at Mosport, Ontario, near Toronto. Most of the other major tracks are in Europe.

When the 1972 world championship series reached the Brands Hatch course in England for the British Grand Prix, the talk of the track was mostly about a young man named Emerson Fittipaldi. In only his second full season of Grand Prix racing, the young Brazilian driver led the world championship standings in his John Player Lotus-Ford. No driver in history had climbed to the front ranks of Grand Prix racing as quickly. He was only 25 years old, but racing experts were already calling the 1970s "the decade of Fittipaldi."

"Racing is measured in generations, defined by the great drivers of a given period," one writer said. Then he named the champions of the past. "Tazio Nuvolari, Juan Fangio, Stirling Moss, Jimmy Clark, Jackie Stewart and now Emerson Fittipaldi—those names represent eras of [Grand Prix] racing which future historians will discuss."

Jackie Stewart, the world champion in 1969 and 1971, had not given up his crown to Fittipaldi, however. Heading into the British race, he was second to the young Brazilian in the point standings. Fittipaldi had 34 and Stewart had 21.

The season had been a miserable one for Stewart.

He had opened well by driving his Tyrrell-Ford to an impressive victory in the Argentina Grand Prix, but then he failed to finish the South African and Spanish races because of mechanical failures. Then he was plagued by ill health, finishing fourth at Monaco. His ailment was diagnosed as a bleeding duodenal ulcer, and his doctor ordered him to take six weeks of complete rest, forcing him to miss two races.

But Stewart had come charging back, winning the French Grand Prix his first time out. Now he needed a victory in the British Grand Prix if he was to have much hope of catching Fittipaldi. Fittipaldi had failed to finish the first race in Argentina. But since then he had won the races in Spain and Belgium, finished second in South Africa and France and run third at Monaco to build a solid lead for the title. Only Stewart, Hulme and Jackie Ickx from the strongest Formula 1 field in history had a chance to overhaul Fittipaldi's lead.

The son of a Brazilian motorsport journalist, Fittipaldi began his racing career in go-karts, then rose quickly through the lower levels of the sport in Brazil. In 1969, Fittipaldi moved to England. With $3,500 of his savings he purchased a Formula-Ford racer to compete in the lower levels of British racing.

His abundant natural ability was noticed by Jim Russell, who headed a famous driving school. Fittipaldi and Russell became partners in the ownership of a Formula 3 car. Although Fittipaldi didn't join the series until mid-season, he won the 1969 British championship. That great performance attracted the attention of Colin Chapman, the head of the fabled

Lotus Racing Team, who signed the young driver for the 1970 Formula 2 season.

Fittipaldi again demonstrated quickly that he was capable of advancement, this time to the big league of racing, the Grand Prix circuit. In mid-season Chapman prepared a Formula 1 car for him, and Fittipaldi

Young Emerson Fittipaldi streaks past a camp of tents and trailers on his way to his first Grand Prix victory at Watkins Glen, New York.

became the number two Lotus driver behind Jochen Rindt, who was on his way to the world championship. Late in the season Rindt had clinched the title when he died in a crash during practice for the Italian GP, and Fittipaldi became the team's top driver. The favorite expression of racing wits had been "Emerson *who?*" But they soon abandoned their jokes when Fittipaldi triumphed in the U.S. Grand Prix at Watkins Glen in his fourth world championship race. Although that victory promised great things for Fittipaldi, the following season (1971) was a bad one for the young driver. The Lotus-Ford had consistent suspension problems, and his inexperience often showed. Then in June 1971, Fittipaldi and his wife Maria-Helena were driving through France to their home in Switzerland when they were involved in a collision with another car. Fittipaldi received three broken ribs and a fractured breast bone. Although he missed one race and drove several others in extreme pain from his injuries, he finished sixth in the world championship standings behind Stewart, who won easily.

By 1972, Fittipaldi was a Brazilian hero equal to Pele, the world's greatest soccer player. Several Brazilian writers, sometimes including his father, followed Emerson's every move in each race. The Grand Prix races in Europe all were televised in Brazil via satellite. They would be watching his performance in Britain in the seventh race of the series.

Jackie Ickx had the pole position in his Ferrari with Fittipaldi beside him on the front row. Peter Revson

Fittipaldi's John Player Special takes a corner at Brands Hatch during the 1972 British Grand Prix.

and Jackie Stewart were in the second row. Tim Schenken and Jean-Pierre Beltoise formed the third row.

At the start of the race, his 12-cylinder Ferrari engine gave Ickx the advantage over Fittipaldi in the drag race to the first turn. Beltoise, Revson and Stewart followed. By the end of four laps in the 76-lap, 201-mile race, Stewart had moved from fifth to third.

Fittipaldi held his black and gold Lotus close to Ickx's bright red Ferrari, moving close on the corners but losing ground on acceleration on the straightaways. The two leaders opened a five-second margin on Stewart by lap 15, but the defending champion made it up again by lap 25.

During practice, the drivers had complained that several spots on the track were covered by small stones. Druids' Corner was especially gritty. Ickx was forced to pull around a slower car at Druids' on lap 25, and Fittipaldi had to swing even wider to avoid a collision. This gave Stewart his chance—he sneaked past Fittipaldi on the inside to take second place.

The three machines resembled the cars on a train as they traveled at high speeds nose-to-tailpipe, with only one second separating them. The knowledgeable British race fans cheered loudly as the baby-faced Ickx, the veteran Stewart and young Fittipaldi staged a brilliant display of Grand Prix driving, each waiting for the other to make the slightest error.

The first sign that Ickx was doomed to failure came when Stewart discovered his visor was covered with oil. A loose hose connection in Ickx's Ferrari was allowing the vital liquid to spray out. But Ickx held on to his lead.

Fittipaldi stayed calmly in third spot, close to Stewart's Tyrrell, waiting for an opportunity to pass. That chance came at Druids' Corner when Stewart slipped sideways on the pebbles. Fittipaldi took over second place.

"I don't know if passing Stewart was such a wise move," Fittipaldi said after the race. "It meant that I was in line to be hit by oil spray from the Ferrari. I had to wipe off my visor occasionally, which isn't easy on a course like Brands Hatch where you need both hands to keep the car on the track."

For 20 laps Fittipaldi had to work hard to keep pace with Ickx through Brands Hatch's tight turns. The performance, quick and consistent, was typical of Fittipaldi's work during the 1972 season. Instead of trying to move ahead of Ickx on a course where passing was difficult, he stayed close behind, ready to pounce if the Belgian ace made an error.

"Of course, Emerson had a superb car which was extremely reliable," Stewart said after the race. "But he drove it with remarkable consistency. He was very fast, but he never placed himself in a situation he couldn't handle. He was always there, running near the front, and I think it demoralized some people."

Because his car was handling erratically, Stewart was unable to keep pace with the front-runners and dropped three seconds behind them. The Ickx-Fittipaldi battle continued until lap 49 when Ickx's Ferrari lost too much oil, and he was forced out of the race. Fittipaldi moved into the lead, five seconds ahead of Stewart. The large number of Scots in the crowd cheered for Stewart to reduce the lead.

Despite his car's handling problem, Stewart made a valiant charge. He drove the two fastest laps of the race, reducing Fittipaldi's lead to two seconds, but he was unable to close the gap any further. Fittipaldi maintained his steady pace in the Lotus, which handled beautifully on the bumpy track. Every time Stewart moved closer with a fast lap, Fittipaldi was informed by his crew and stretched his lead with a fast lap of his own.

"That type of race was very difficult on the nerves," Stewart said. "Emerson had to stay very cool in the long race with Ickx and then again when I was closing on him. But he did it, which is remarkable considering that he hasn't been around Grand Prix racing for too long."

At the finish, Fittipaldi's margin was five seconds. When he crossed the finish line and took the checkered flag, Fittipaldi's team boss Colin Chapman jubilantly threw his hat in the air.

The victory added nine points to Fittipaldi's total, giving him 43 after seven of twelve races. Stewart's six points for second place boosted him to 27 points. Only a complete Fittipaldi collapse could deprive the young Brazilian of the world title.

Both Fittipaldi and Stewart dropped out early in the German Grand Prix at Nurburgring, which was won by Ickx. Fittipaldi then clinched the championship with victories in the Dutch and Italian races which gave him five wins and 61 points for the season. Stewart closed out the season impressively with wins in Canada and the United States to finish second with 45 points.

Assessing his championship season, Fittipaldi considered the British race as pivotal in his march to the crown. "The track was extremely rough and the pattern of the race, especially the battles with Ickx and Stewart, made the pace very fast," Fittipaldi said. "When the Lotus stood up to that terrific pounding, I knew I had a very tough, reliable car. It probably was the most competitive race of the season."

The loquacious Stewart placed the Grand Prix season in its proper perspective: "The combination of an excellent car and a brilliant young driver won the championship," Stewart said. "And I think the rest of us may have great difficulty getting it away from him."

World champion Fittipaldi (right) has a laugh with former world champion Jackie Stewart at the beginning of the 1973 season.

4

The Bruce and Denny Show

The cars were huge, wedge-shaped, bright orange monsters, built with smooth, clean lines. The drivers were two men from New Zealand—the smiling, easygoing Bruce McLaren, a genius in design, construction, testing and driving; and the quiet, introverted Denis Hulme, an extraordinarily strong and competitive driver.

The series was the Canadian-American Challenge Cup for Group 7 sports racing cars, but for three seasons, from 1967 to 1969, it had been known as "The Bruce and Denny Show."

Auto racing is a fickle business. One year's winning car often is next year's loser, so racing dynasties are difficult to construct. Although the top teams in several types of racing are consistent contenders year after year, most of them have their ups and downs—sometimes several races or even entire seasons when their cars won't go quite fast enough or must drop out because of mechanical failures. In racing so many things can go wrong that consistency is almost impossible to achieve.

But in the Can-Am series, Team McLaren was different. In 1967, '68 and '69, McLaren and Hulme won 20 of 23 races and earned 13 second-place finishes. No team in racing history produced a record which came even close to matching that performance.

Especially noteworthy in that streak was the 1969 season when the Can-Am expanded from a six-race autumn series to eleven events run from June to November. Team McLaren entered two McLaren M8B models powered by 427 cubic inch Chevrolet engines. (Some rivals claimed the engines were illegally modified to a 480 cubic inch displacement, but McLaren merely laughed at the accusation.)

The powerful McLaren team failed to frighten away potential rivals. The eleven races in 1969 had average fields of 25 cars, several driven by top international stars. However, no driver-car combination was capable of beating the "orange brutes." Team McLaren won all eleven races. McLaren himself was victorious in six events and finished second three times to collect the Can-Am championship with 165 points. He received $160,950 in prize money. Denis Hulme, the other McLaren driver, won the other five races, was second in five more and was runner-up in the standings with 160 points. His prize money totaled $151,134.

When asked to explain the reasons for his team's great success, McLaren offered no mysterious solutions.

"Just old-fashioned hard work by everyone connected with the team," he said. "There's nothing very fancy about us."

McLaren had been a top sports car racer in New Zealand and had completed three years of university engineering studies. At 21, he moved to Grand Prix racing in Europe sponsored by a scholarship which

Denis Hulme watches as crew members push Bruce McLaren's car out onto the track.

sent promising New Zealand drivers into big league competition. McLaren drove for the Cooper team for several seasons, but his dream was to organize a racing team of his own.

In 1964, Team McLaren was formed when McLaren joined forces with Teddy Mayer, who had a Yale University law degree. Mayer had managed the

racing career of his brother Tim, but Tim was killed in a crash in 1964 and Teddy became McLaren's partner in Team McLaren.

McLaren's main interest was sports cars. The first McLaren Group 7 model appeared in 1965 and was an instant success. McLaren's engineering background allowed him to participate in the design and construction of the cars. And he excelled as a test driver because his engineering background helped him detect the smallest flaw in a car.

"I certainly wouldn't call myself an innovator in car design," McLaren said. "We started with a solid car and slowly improved it. We were fortunate in hiring some excellent people to work on our team."

When the Can-Am series was initiated in 1966, McLaren and another New Zealander, Chris Amon, drove the team cars. Although the machines were competitive, the team failed to win a race. Before the 1966 season ended, McLaren was deep into construction of the cars for the 1967 series. The result was the first orange brute, the McLaren M6A. McLaren hired Hulme as co-driver, and the Bruce and Denny Show made its debut.

Team McLaren won five of six Can-Am races in 1967. Hulme won three events; McLaren claimed the points title with two wins and two seconds. It was a big year for the two drivers. Hulme won the world championship Formula 1 series driving for the Brabham team, and the first McLaren Grand Prix car appeared, driven by McLaren. In 1968, Hulme was Can-Am champ with three wins and a second, while McLaren won one race and was second twice.

A Team McLaren "secret" was to be well prepared for the first race. The 1969 cars were on the test track in January. By the time they appeared for the series opener at Mosport Park, Ontario, in June, the machines were ready to race.

"For this year, we'll have slightly wider tires, slightly more power, better brakes and a few minor body changes," said McLaren. "Also, our cars will be better prepared. We should be at least two seconds faster on most tracks because of these improvements."

The 1969 Can-Am entry list contained top Grand Prix drivers Chris Amon, John Surtees and Jo Siffert; U.S. stars Chuck Parsons, Lothar Motschenbacher, Peter Revson and Dan Gurney; and Canadians George Eaton and John Cordts. Many teams entered McLaren-designed cars which were constructed and marketed by Trojan Cars of England.

McLaren and Hulme quickly demonstrated that Team McLaren was indeed well prepared for the 1969 series. They earned the front row positions on the starting grid for the Mosport race. Driving a new McLaren because the Chaparral he was slated to handle for Texan Jim Hall wasn't ready, John Surtees battled McLaren for the early lead. But when Surtees' car overheated, Bruce gradually took command.

Hulme settled into second place and had to hold off Gurney for 50 laps until Gurney's suspension broke. Although Hulme caught and passed McLaren for a few laps, at the finish McLaren was one second ahead.

"I suspect that we can all look forward to seeing a great deal of McLaren tailpipe in this series," Gurney commented after the race.

Hulme and McLaren fight for first place in the 1969 Can-Am race at Mosport, Ontario. Although Hulme is ahead, McLaren won by a second.

Surtees, however, wasn't satisfied with that role. In the second race at Le Circuit, Quebec, he pushed McLaren for the lead in the first 20 laps in a splendid battle of high speed maneuvers. Even when Hulme passed them both to take the lead, the McLaren-Surtees scramble continued. On lap 22, the cars touched in a hairpin corner, and Surtees was forced to the pits to have his rear body section repaired. At the finish Hulme was in front, a few yards ahead of McLaren.

Another New Zealander, Chris Amon, arrived with a Ferrari 612 to supply a strong challenge for Team

McLaren at Watkins Glen, New York, in the third race. Although McLaren won and Hulme was second, Amon finished 23 seconds back of the leader to indicate the "orange brute" romp might not be easy.

At Edmonton, McLaren, Amon and Hulme scrapped for the lead for 34 laps. Then Team McLaren had its first casualty of the series—McLaren had to drop out because of a piston failure. When Bruce exited, Hulme quickly pushed his car to a five-second lead which the determined Amon was unable to reduce. Surtees had made his first start in the new Chaparral but finished fourth.

Asked if he thought the McLaren domination was hurting the series and killing spectator interest, Hulme replied: "No way! I think the fans come to the Can-Am races to see us get beat. What are we supposed to do? Deliberately lose a few races?"

Hulme was in top form at Mid-Ohio, winning the race by almost a minute over McLaren. Amon offered strong competition at Elkhart Lake until his Ferrari ran out of gas seven laps from the finish. The orange cars crossed the finish line in a wave with McLaren one-tenth of a second in front of Hulme.

Bridgehampton, New York, supplied a chance for Hulme to score a win by less than a second over McLaren. At one point, Hulme dropped back from the lead to supply a slipstream "tow" for Amon, but the Ferrari dropped out.

All season the Team McLaren entourage had included a third car, ready to race if anything happened to the other two machines. When the Can-Am reached Michigan International Speedway,

Dan Gurney was in the cockpit of the third car. Although he started at the back of the grid, he swept through the pack to finish third behind McLaren and Hulme.

"I don't mind McLaren and Hulme taking all the meat and potatoes off the platter," said George Eaton, the young Canadian who was running strongly in the series. "But do they have to bring along Gurney to clean up the scraps?"

When the series moved west to California, the results remained the same. McLaren won at Laguna Seca with Hulme second. Mario Andretti in a McLaren-Ford ran a strong fourth.

McLaren was involved in the team's only serious incident at Riverside. He was running second to Hulme on lap 35 when a broken suspension sent his car into a wild spin on a corner. The car slid up a small bank where it struck a track marshal, bounced into a guardrail and back on to the track. McLaren wasn't injured but the marshal had two broken legs. Hulme won the race by more than a lap over Parsons, with Andretti third.

Only one race stood in the way of an unprecedented Team McLaren sweep of the Can-Am series—the first event ever staged at the new Texas International Speedway. McLaren drove the spare team car because of the severe damage to his own machine in the Riverside crash.

Andretti pushed his McLaren-Ford into the lead at the start, and the spectators figured an upset was possible. However, that notion lasted only five laps until Andretti's engine blew up, and McLaren and

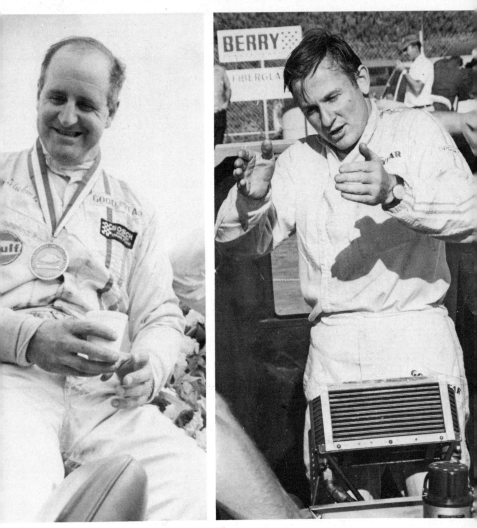

**Hulme relaxes after a race while Bruce McLaren intently discusses the
championship cars he was designing and building.**

Hulme swept into the lead. McLaren ran in front for the remainder of the race. Hulme had his first non-finish of the year when his engine failed eleven laps from the end, and young Eaton finished second.

McLaren was philosophical about the series sweep after the Texas race. "It's extremely pleasing to our team to win every race," he said. "We're enjoying it while we can, though, because nothing lasts forever, especially in auto racing."

McLaren's statement was prophetic. In June 1970, while testing the team's cars for the Can-Am series at the Goodwood track in England, McLaren was killed in a crash. The rear body section of his car lifted at 140 miles per hour, and the car went out of control.

However, the strong organization which McLaren had built carried on the team tradition in the Can-Am. Hulme won the title in 1970 and team driver Peter Revson was champion in 1971. The tradition of excellence which Bruce McLaren established endured.

5

The Virtuoso's Last Season

From the time the Nurburgring track near Bonn, Germany, opened in 1927, auto racers have had a love-hate relationship with it. The 14.2-mile road circuit, one of the world's most beautiful, winds through a pine forest in the Eifel Mountains. The narrow ribbon of asphalt climbs, falls and twists through the green, rolling countryside.

Drivers detested Nurburgring's bumpy surface caused by the frost of winter, and the several sharp inclines on the course that actually sent cars flying at high speeds. There were more than 150 turns and curves in the course, making it extremely difficult to commit to memory. Each year the drivers studied the track as carefully as possible, testing for new bumps and looking for the fastest line through the corners.

However, Nurburgring offered a mighty challenge

to the great drivers, most of whom regarded the course as the ultimate test of driving skill. To go quickly and consistently at the "Ring" was racing's supreme satisfaction.

On a warm August afternoon in 1957, some 250,000 spectators were scattered around the track. Many camped for the weekend among the pines in the infield to see the German Grand Prix, one of the world championship's most glamorous events.

Although the race always attracted large crowds, the 1957 race had a special element of interest. The Ferrari team of Italy had mounted an impressive troika of young drivers in Luigi Musso of Italy and Peter Collins and Mike Hawthorn of England. The series also included such great drivers as Stirling Moss, Jean Behra, Harry Schell and Tony Brooks. But the man who set the standard was Juan Manuel Fangio.

Juan Fangio! That name was as magical in auto racing history as Babe Ruth was in baseball, Bill Tilden in tennis and Bobby Jones in golf. Most experts regarded Fangio as the finest driver in the history of Grand Prix racing.

"The best classroom of all time for a driver, I'm convinced, was a spot about two car lengths behind Juan Manuel Fangio," said Stirling Moss, the superb British driver. "I learned more there than I ever did anywhere else."

Fangio was born into poverty in Balcarce, Argentina, the son of an Italian immigrant plasterer. In 1922, at eleven years of age, Fangio went to work as a mechanic. When he was 25, he drove his first race on a local dirt track in a converted taxi. Although the car

The legendary Juan Manuel Fangio takes a quick gulp of soda during a refueling stop in the 1949 Grand Prix at Monza, Italy.

fell apart, Fangio rebuilt it and quickly established a reputation as a fearless competitor.

Fangio's first important victory came in the 1940 Gran Premio International del Norte, a 5,932-mile, open-road race through the Andes mountains from

Buenos Aires, Argentina, to Lima, Peru, and back. The race lasted 13 days. Fangio, driving alone without relief in a souped-up 1939 Chevrolet, drove nine hours each day, often over unpaved mountain roads that were scarcely more than cattle tracks. He won the race by a wide margin and earned fame all over South America.

Fangio continued to win regularly in his Chevrolet. During World War II racing was suspended due to lack of gasoline and rubber. Fangio returned to his garage. After the war, Juan Peron came to power as Argentina's dictator president. One of his dreams was to make Buenos Aires the auto racing capital of the world. European racing's biggest names were invited for races, but the Peron government also wanted a group of Argentinian drivers to compete against them. Fangio was 35 at the time, a roughneck, unpolished driver in comparison to the smooth Europeans. But he studied the styles of the visitors and absorbed a great deal of racing knowledge.

With government backing, Fangio went to Europe in 1949 where he won six of ten Grand Prix races in a Maserati, increasing his standing as a national hero.

The official world driving championship was inaugurated in 1950. Fangio lost the title to Nino Farina. But in 1951, with a large entourage of Spanish journalists and broadcasters covering his every move, Fangio won the title in a Maserati. A year later he crashed at Monza in Italy, broke his neck and missed almost the entire season.

Alberto Ascari in a Ferrari won the world title in 1952 and 1953, but for the next few years that laurel

Driving a Maserati, Fangio raises the dust as he rounds a turn.

became Fangio's personal property. The reckless rowdy of the Argentina dirt tracks had transformed himself into a smooth, prudent Formula 1 driver, learning never to push himself or his car beyond their limits.

Fangio won the world title in 1954, dividing the season between Maserati and Mercedes cars. He piloted a Mercedes to the crown in 1955 and won in a Ferrari in 1956. In 1957 he again drove a Maserati for what was to be his last full season of competition. Many of Fangio's friends had been killed in crashes during his years on the track, and he brooded about those who had died. But nothing affected his superiority behind the wheel of a Formula 1 car.

Maserati had constructed a streamlined car with a lightweight space-frame chassis for the 1957 season and had increased the power of its six-cylinder engine to 270 horsepower. Other cars had been improved, too, but only Fangio's Maserati ran consistently well. He won in Argentina, Monaco and France and finished second to Moss in Britain.

Thus, Fangio had a solid lead towards his fifth title going into the German Grand Prix at Nurburgring. On this track, however, Fangio faced a handicap to the Ferraris. Because the race was 310 miles (22 laps) long, the Maserati required a pit stop for fuel and tires, while the Ferraris of Hawthorn, Collins and Musso could go the distance with no stops. Yet Fangio demonstrated in practice that he wasn't ready to concede anything. He earned the pole position, beating the Nurburgring record he had set the year before in a Ferrari by 15 seconds.

"I'm a minute behind before the race starts," Fangio said on the starting grid, referring to the time required for his pit stop.

Because of the pit stop, Fangio's fuel tank was only half full at the start which gave him an advantage in weight over the full-tanked Ferraris. Hawthorn and Collins passed Fangio at the start, and the three cars ran at close quarters during the first three laps. Then Fangio moved in front and, pushing the big red car as hard as he could, built a 28-second lead by the halfway point when he made his pit stop.

While the gasoline was pumped into the car, Hawthorn and Collins roared past the pits. When Fangio returned to the track, he was almost 50 seconds

behind and had the additional handicap of full fuel
tanks. The gap seemed simply too much for the
46-year-old Fangio to make up in the remaining
twelve laps.

Some spectators said that Fangio held back after his
pit stop for a few laps to lull the Ferrari team into a
false sense of security. When the Ferrari timers discovered that Fangio wasn't gaining much, they flashed the
"slow down" sign to Hawthorn and Collins. When
Fangio came past his pit, 45 seconds behind the
leaders, his crew gave him the nod. The ruse had
worked. Now Fangio poured on the speed. Two laps
were run before the Ferrari crew could tell its drivers
that Fangio had speeded up and was gaining fast.

Hawthorn and Collins did everything possible to
protect their lead. Collins turned in a lap of 9 minutes,
28.9 seconds, a new course record, passing Hawthorn
and taking the lead. But on that lap, Fangio gained
five seconds, running even faster.

On ten consecutive laps, Fangio broke the course
record as he took large bites from the Ferrari margin
each time around. As one man in the pits said that
day: "Fangio is possessed by the devil himself."

Fangio was gaining on the Ferraris at the rate of six
seconds per lap. On lap 20, he lowered the Nurburgring record to 9:17.4 and gained eleven seconds on
the leader, Hawthorn. When the cars crossed the line
to start lap 21, Fangio was sitting on the exhaust pipes
of the Ferraris. The crowd cheered wildly for him.

Going through the famous Karussel turn on the 21st
lap, Fangio nipped ahead of second-place Collins by
going low on the inside. The Maserati's rear wheel

threw a stone that broke Collins' goggles. Fangio's next target was Hawthorn, and before the lap was completed, he blew past the British star into the lead.

"The car was producing every bit of power it had, and I was driving it to the best of my ability," said Hawthorn after the race. "But there was just nothing, not a single thing, I could do about holding Fangio off."

Fangio had a four-second lead on Hawthorn when they crossed the finish line. The victory clinched the fifth world driving championship for the stout, quiet man from Argentina.

Fangio takes the winner's checkered flag in the 1957 German Grand Prix after one of the greatest driving performances in history.

The huge crowd shouted Fangio's name repeatedly when he pulled into the pits at the end of the race. They had watched genius in the cockpit of a racing car. Fangio wasn't a man who usually drove at the limit, but on that day he had pushed the Maserati to the brink and held it there for the last 150 miles.

When he climbed out of the car, Fangio was trembling. He said, "I'll never do that again as long as I live."

When the 1957 season ended, Maserati announced that the team was dropping out of racing because the cost had become too great. At the start of the 1958 season, Fangio said that he was dropping out, too. He planned to ease out of the sport which had made him rich and famous, driving only a few selected races.

The 1958 French Grand Prix at Rheims was his last race. He drove a privately built Maserati and finished fourth when the clutch burned out near the end.

Fangio practiced for the Indianapolis 500 and the Le Mans 24-hour endurance race that year, then withdrew at the last minute. Some detractors claimed he was a "cheese champion," and that he had lost his courage. Fangio never replied to such unthinking criticism. He said that neither his age nor the many deaths of drivers in the 1958 season influenced his decision.

"I've attained all the goals any man could want in auto racing," Fangio said. "If I could win another world championship, what value would it have for me?"

However, the debate of whether Fangio had lost his heart for racing raged on. One year he attended the

Italian Grand Prix at Monza. During the award ceremony, he said, "It was a great race. No one was killed."

Fangio retired to his successful automobile dealership in Buenos Aires, where he said he would never race again or even attend a race as a spectator. "I couldn't go to a race again, even to watch," he told a reporter. "Too many of my great racing brothers are dead, and if I went to a race, it would be too painful for me."

But the pull of the track was too strong. He made a trip to Europe during the 1959 season and watched several events. He had little to say when questioned by reporters.

For years, some claimed that Fangio had quit racing because he was afraid. But the 250,000 spectators who watched him at Nurburgring that day in 1957 knew differently.

6

Twenty-Four Hours to Glory

David versus Goliath!

That was the way the European press built up the battle between the Ferrari and Ford racing teams in the 1967 Le Mans race. Le Mans was a grueling, 24-hour endurance race over an 8.3-mile course of public roads in the farming country of mid-western France. It was the most famous of a series of endurance races for the World Manufacturers' Championship— in this series, the big prize went to the winning car, not to the drivers.

The Ferrari team played David to Ford's Goliath. Ferraris were made by a little Italian auto factory with approximately 500 employees. The plant produced fewer than 1,000 expensive, hand-made sports cars each year. The legendary Enzo Ferrari had made his cars and his racing teams internationally famous from the early days of the sport. By contrast, the American Ford Motor Company had nearly 400,000 employees and was one of the world's industrial giants. Millions of automobiles rolled off its assembly lines each year.

Some considered the Le Mans competition between Ferrari and Ford a contest between the craftsmanship of the old European world and the advanced technological knowledge of the New World. Others saw the contrasting motives of the two companies. Enzo Ferrari raced cars because it was something he had always done, something he wanted to do. Ford had invested a huge budget, rumored to be $8,000,000, on the development of the Mark IV cars for Le Mans, hoping that success on the race track would bring even greater success in the sale of its passenger cars.

This was the third year of competition between the two great auto companies. Ford had mounted a large effort to win the series in 1965. But Ferrari swept the series title and won the first three positions at Le Mans when the Fords all suffered mechanical failure.

In 1966, Ford swept the Ferraris aside at Le Mans and ended the Italian team's string of six consecutive triumphs. The Ford driving teams of Bruce McLaren and Chris Amon, and Ken Miles and Denis Hulme claimed the first two positions.

So 1967 would be the deciding year. Both teams launched large construction and development programs for the series. Ford driver Ken Miles was killed in a test of a Ford model called the "J-car." Seeking to protect its drivers, Ford modified the J-car extensively, adding a heavy roll cage around the cockpit. And to gain more speed, Ford developed a 7-liter, 530 horsepower engine. The result was the Mark IV, a big, solid racing machine.

Ferrari constructed a new model, called the P-4, which carried a 4-liter V-12 engine that produced 450 horsepower. Although the P-4 was less powerful than Ford's Mark IV, it also weighed 800 pounds less.

The 1967 manufacturers' series began with a 24-hour race in Daytona, Florida. Ferrari claimed the first round of the battle. The driving team of Chris Amon and Lorenzo Bandini won as the Ferrari's P-4 swept the first three finishing positions. The Fords vanished with assorted breakdowns. The Ferrari team missed the second race at Sebring (also in Florida) to concentrate on preparation for the European races. Driving Mark IV's, Mario Andretti and Bruce McLaren finished first, and A. J. Foyt and Lloyd Ruby finished second. (Endurance cars are usually driven by two-man teams; while one is driving, the other is resting in the pit area.)

The stage was set for Le Mans. The mighty Ford team entered seven cars, four new Mark IV models and three Mark II's, all painted in different bright colors. The Ferrari factory countered with four P-4's, painted bright red and carrying the famous "prancing horse" insignia. In addition, four strong Ferraris were prepared by private entrants. The only other serious contender was the Chaparral of Texan Jim Hall.

Ford had signed 14 of the world's top drivers to handle the cars. The teams for the Mark IV's were A. J. Foyt, who had won the Indianapolis 500 two weeks earlier, and Dan Gurney; Bruce McLaren and Mark Donohue; Mario Andretti and Lucien Bianchi;

and Lloyd Ruby and Denis Hulme. Drivers of the less competitive Mark II's included Frank Gardner, Roger McCluskey and Ronnie Bucknum. The Ford line-up was certainly expensive, but some experts thought many of the drivers inexperienced. Foyt, Andretti and others were used to racing on oval tracks in Indianapo-

The Ford Mark IV, an $8-million car designed for speed and endurance . . .

lis-type cars and had had little or no experience in road racing.

"The fact that some Ford drivers have very little road-racing experience and little background in driving at night has to help us," said one Ferrari driver. "They'll find that Le Mans is a course you must know very well, especially with all those slow cars."

The Ferrari team lost two of its best drivers before Le Mans. Lorenzo Bandini was killed in a crash during the Monaco Grand Prix, and John Surtees suddenly left the team. The P-4 factory cars were handled by Chris Amon and Nino Vaccarella; Ludovico Scarfiotti and Mike Parkes; Gunter Klass and John Sutcliffe; and Willy Mairesse and Jean Beurlys.

The Le Mans course was roughly rectangular and was made up of paved, two-lane country roads. Its most famous section was the long Mulsanne straight, which was more than two miles in length and provided an unequaled opportunity for cars to hit top speed.

The big Ferraris and Fords were not the only cars that would run the race. There would also be smaller cars with top speeds of 125 miles per hour or less competing for "class" awards. Some of the drivers would be inexperienced, too. A Ford or Ferrari going

. . . **and looking like a wingless airplane.**

200 miles per hour on the long straight might encounter one of these inexperienced drivers trying to pass at 125—causing danger and delay. There would be 55 cars in all.

At 4 o'clock on Saturday afternoon, the cars were lined up in front of the pits for the special "Le Mans" start. The drivers stood poised on the side of the track. When the flag fell, the drivers sprinted to their cars,

**The cars head out of the pits as
the 1967 Le Mans 24-hour classic
begins. The Foyt-Gurney Ford is
Number 1 (right center).**

buckled themselves into the seats, started their engines
and sped away on the toughest 24 hours in motor
racing.

At the end of the first lap, Ronnie Bucknum's Ford
Mark II was in the lead, and Fords held four of the
first five positions. Ferrari's race strategy soon became
clear. The P-4 drivers didn't try to match the pace of
the more powerful Fords, but stayed in a position to
challenge, running easily. They planned to concentrate on finishing the race, expecting the Ford engines
to break down sooner or later.

Trouble hit the Ford team early as three of the seven
cars were forced to make unscheduled pit stops during
the first hour for mechanical repairs. When most cars
made their first pit stops at 5 p.m., Ronnie Bucknum
was leading in a Ford Mark II, followed by Gurney
and McLaren in Mark IV's, Mike Spence driving the
Chaparral and Vaccarella in the first Ferrari. When
the Fords pitted, Spence wheeled the big white Chaparral into the lead. He pitted at 5:17, and Foyt drove
the bright red Number 1 Ford into first place.

Foyt was a tough, outspoken, hot-tempered Texan

who had made his reputation on the U.S. dirt tracks and ovals. Foyt had never seen the Le Mans track before his practice laps, and he had seldom raced on road courses. He made an unusual driving partner for Dan Gurney, a quiet studious man who had started out by racing sports cars in the United States and gone on to win several Grands Prix.

As darkness fell over the course, Gurney and Foyt drove on, extending their lead steadily in a beautifully controlled performance. After six hours they were followed by McLaren and Donohue in a Ford, Spence and Phil Hill in the Chaparral, and the Ferraris of Parkes and Scarfiotti, and Amon and Vaccarella.

Amon was the first of the leaders to drop out. When his P-4 had a flat tire and he was unable to change it on the course, he tried driving the car back to the pits. The friction of the tire rubbing against the wheel set fire to the car, and Amon scrambled out to watch the entire auto consumed by the flames.

Then it was Ford's turn for trouble. The Hawkins-Bucknum car, a Mark II, which was running strongly, needed a two-hour pit stop to repair a fuel line. Then Ruby ran his Mark IV off the course and into a sand bank where it was firmly stuck. But there were still five Fords in the running, most of them in strong position.

At 3:15 a.m. Sunday as the race neared the halfway point, the Fords were still in command. But then the situation changed dramatically in a few seconds. Running in second place behind the Gurney-Foyt car, Lucien Bianchi brought his Ford into the pits for fuel and new brake pads. Bianchi's teammate Mario Andretti took over the driving chores and roared out of the pits, up the hill towards the first turn. When he touched the brakes, the right front brake grabbed and the car went into a wild spin. It hit the wall, spun across the track, smacked a dirt bank and came to a stop in the middle of the pavement. Andretti scrambled out of the car and ran to the side of the track.

Only a few seconds behind Andretti, Roger McCluskey, in a Mark II, roared over the hill. When he saw the battered hulk of Andretti's car, he swerved around it and crashed. "If Mario was still in the car and I hit him, I'd have killed him for sure," McCluskey said. "So I had to put my car into the wall."

McCluskey's car bounced off the wall and the bank, also spinning to a stop in the middle of the track. Another Ford Mark II, driven by Schlesser, appeared on the accident scene and it, too, spun into the wall. Thanks to the recent improvements in the Fords' construction, none of the three drivers was seriously injured, although Andretti had bruised ribs and a cut knee. But the situation was looking grim for Ford. Only two of their seven cars were in strong position, and only three were in the race at all.

Later the third-place Chaparral dropped out. Now the competition was strictly between Ford and Ferrari. Gurney and Foyt had a five-lap lead over the Parkes-Scarfiotti and Mairesse-Beurlys Ferraris. McLaren and Donohue, in the only other challenging Ford, were a hard-charging fourth, attempting to make up time lost to have their clutch repaired. Then McLaren lost the rear body section off his car. He drove a slow lap, retrieved the pieces and returned to the pits. The

Dan Gurney and A. J. Foyt chat during their victory celebration.

crew riveted and taped it together. But when he rejoined the race, he was 16 laps behind the third-place Ferrari.

Out of seven Fords, five had dropped out, and one was too far back to catch up. Only Foyt and Gurney were still in contention. The Ferrari drivers were waiting for that last car to fall back, too. The first

Ferrari was 40 miles behind Foyt and Gurney, but if the Ford had to stop for even minor repairs, that 40 miles could be made up in less than 20 minutes. But the Ferrari wait was in vain. Foyt and Gurney slowed to an easy pace through the closing hours of the race and changed places frequently. At the finish they were four laps ahead of the Parkes-Scarfiotti Ferrari.

As Foyt drove the bright red car across the finish line at 4 p.m. Sunday, the crowd of nearly 300,000 and the jubilant Ford pit crews cheered. Gurney jumped on the fender of the car and Foyt drove it to the victory circle.

Foyt and Gurney had completed 387.6 laps, a distance of 3,249.6 miles, almost 250 miles farther than the record set by the Ford Mark II in 1966. Their average speed was 135.483 miles per hour.

"Before that race, many Europeans regarded Foyt as the definitive oval-only American driver," Bruce McLaren said. "But at Le Mans, he did a great job. He was just as fast and consistent as any road racer."

"That's some ol' car," drawled Foyt after he and Gurney sprayed everyone in sight with champagne from the winner's platform. "I'm certain it would run another 24 hours without stopping."

Ford had won again, but not before some heart-stopping moments. The company dropped out of the World Manufacturers' Championship at the end of the 1967 season, and endurance racing fell into a decline. But the Number 1 Mark IV model, which carried Gurney and Foyt so far and so fast, occupies a prominent place in the Ford museum as one of the greatest racing machines ever constructed.

7

The Flying Scot

Winning consistently was something which Jimmy Clark had done from the time he made his Formula 1 debut with the Lotus team in 1960. He had teamed up with Colin Chapman, a retired driver who was becoming famous as the designer and builder of the great Lotus racing cars. In the next few years, Clark and Chapman formed one of the greatest driver-constructor teams in Grand Prix racing history. Although Clark had little technical expertise, he was able to tell Chapman exactly how the car handled in test runs, and Chapman was able to translate Clark's explanations into mechanical improvements. Then Jimmy went out and drove the car in competition, making the most of its strengths.

Clark quickly learned the Grand Prix ropes in his first two seasons with Lotus. He had some high finishes, but it wasn't until 1962 that he won his first race, the Belgian GP. He was arriving at the top just when Grand Prix racing needed a new superstar. The great Juan Fangio had retired in 1958, and Stirling Moss, who had replaced Fangio as top driver, was critically injured in a crash in early 1962. Clark, a native of Scotland, was the man to replace them.

Jimmy came close to winning the world championship in 1962, losing it to Graham Hill in the final race of the season. In 1963 he swept the crown by winning a record seven races. He lost the title to John Surtees of England in 1964, but roared back in 1965 to take his second driving championship. He also won the Indianapolis 500 in 1965 with the first rear-engined car ever to win that race.

Then the specifications for Formula 1 cars were changed for the 1966 season. Maximum engine displacement was increased from 1.5 liters to 3 liters. The Brabham team was the only one prepared for the 1966 formula switch, and Brabham won his third world title. But Colin Chapman was working on the new Lotus 49 with a great Cosworth-Ford engine. It appeared that Lotus would be back at the top in 1967.

When the season started, the new Lotus wasn't quite ready. Clark drove an older car in the first two races. Then the Lotus 49 made a sensational debut in its first race. Driven by Jim Clark, it won the Dutch GP, a rare achievement for a car not long off the drawing board.

But the 1967 Grand Prix season was not a good one for Jimmy Clark. The new Lotus 49 included too many innovations. The car proved to be unreliable,

Jim Clark after driving the Lotus 49 to its first victory, in the 1967 Dutch Grand Prix.

and a variety of mechanical faults sidelined Clark in several races as he sought his third world driving championship.

When the car functioned correctly, it was very fast. Clark scored one more impressive victory in the Grand Prix of Great Britain. But while he was battling mechanical gremlins in other races, steady Denis Hulme of New Zealand and Jack Brabham of Australia, driving the Brabham-Repco cars, built a solid lead at the top of the championship point standings.

Clark was more frustrated than depressed by the car's failures. He realized a new machine just needed development time to cure the problems.

"I know that the 49 will be one of the greatest Grand Prix cars ever," said Clark during the Canadian GP, the eighth race of the eleven-race series. "But little things are hurting us now. We just have to work hard and iron them out. It's a little frustrating to realize how close we are to having a car that will win consistently."

When the drivers traveled to Monza for the Italian GP, Hulme, the steady New Zealander, had a firm grip on the title with 43 points, and Brabham had 34. Clark was third with 23 points. Points were awarded on a 9-6-4-3-2-1 basis to the first six finishers in each race. With only three events remaining on the schedule (Italy, United States and Mexico), Clark's hopes of winning were very slim. To have any chance, he would have to win at Monza.

Of all the tracks on the Grand Prix circuit, Clark disliked Monza the most. The 3.6-mile track was flat and uninteresting, but speeds there were the highest. The cars tended to separate into fast and slow groups, running in bunches. There was much slipstreaming, in which one car sat close behind another and received a "tow" from the vacuum created by the car in front.

"Monza isn't much of a drivers' circuit," Clark said. "It's a straight speed track, and the turns are either very fast or very slow. I don't like it very much."

Yet the Lotus 49 with the strong Cosworth-Ford engine was perfectly suited for the Monza track. In practice, Clark earned the pole position with a lap at 145.33 miles per hour, more than 13 miles per hour quicker than the old record.

The starting order indicated that the race would be brutally competitive. The first nine cars had qualified within 1.8 seconds of each other. Clark, Brabham and

Bruce McLaren would start in the front row. Chris Amon and Dan Gurney would be in row two. Then came Hulme, Jackie Stewart and Graham Hill in row three, with John Surtees, in the new Honda, and Ludovico Scarfiotti behind them. Jimmy Clark faced a tough battle to keep his world title hopes alive.

The format called for the cars to form up on the mock grid and move up to the starting grid for a 10-second pause before the start. However, as the cars were moving to the starting grid, the starter dropped the flag. Clark and several other drivers weren't prepared. As a result, Gurney, Brabham and Hill all led Clark at the end of the first lap.

The field quickly separated into two groups. Gurney led for the first five laps, followed closely by Clark, Hulme, Brabham and Graham Hill. Then Gurney's engine failed, and Clark went ahead, racing three other cars at close quarters for several laps. They slipstreamed on the straights and tried to pass him on the corners.

On lap twelve, Clark felt a strange vibration from the rear of the car. Brabham, who was close behind, saw that Clark's rear tire was swollen, which indicated a slow-leaking puncture. Brabham took a big risk, moving out of the regular line at 150 miles per hour, to wave at Clark and warn him of the problem. Clark pulled into the pits to have the wheel changed.

When Clark rejoined the race after a 90-second pit stop, he was one lap and 20 seconds behind Hulme— nearly two minutes altogether. Some drivers had claimed that Clark wasn't a "tiger," a driver who drove flat out when the situation appeared hopeless.

Clark's long, sleek Lotus 49 during his big victory in the 1967 British Grand Prix. Soon after he drove his greatest race at Monza.

On that day, however, Clark growled with the best of them.

After 18 laps, Clark had made up only 20 seconds on the leaders. He was still a full lap behind, last in the field. With 38 laps of the 68-lap race to go and a full lap to make up, many drivers would have given up and driven easily. Not Clark on that day! He pushed his foot to the floor and took off in pursuit of the front-runners. At the front of the pack, Hill, Hulme and Brabham had been staging a lively battle. Then Hulme's engine blew a gasket and he dropped out. Graham Hill, Clark's Lotus teammate, quickly opened a lead on Brabham.

Clark consistently lowered the race lap record until he had matched his qualifying speed. On lap 50 he was in eighth place. Hill was now in the lead, 53 seconds in front of Brabham. Surtees was third, 68 seconds behind. Clark had moved to within 30 seconds of

Surtees, but he was still nearly a lap (3.6 miles) behind Hill. Then in a magnificent driving display Clark cut Surtees' lead to 12 seconds in only five laps.

"What we were watching that day was a virtuoso drive which no other driver has equaled or will ever be able to surpass," said Colin Chapman. "It was one of those rare drives in Jimmy's career when he drove flat out. Usually, he left a little in reserve, but at Monza that day, he used up all his resources."

The entire complexion of the race changed on lap 57 when the engine in Hill's Lotus blew up. Suddenly the race became a three-way fight between Brabham, Surtees and Clark. When the three cars rolled past the pits on lap 60, Brabham led Surtees by three seconds with Clark only two seconds behind that.

A murmur ran through the crowd predicting that Clark would be in front the next time around. All eyes were on the sweeping "Parabolica Curve" near the main straight. Clark rounded the curve first. He had taken the lead! Brabham and Surtees were battling for second, and it appeared that Clark was on his way to an astounding victory.

With three laps remaining in the race, Clark's lead was three seconds. Surtees had passed Brabham and was in second. But when the leaders came around to start lap 67, Clark had given up a second of his margin and was pointing frantically at the gauges on his dashboard. As the cars disappeared on the final lap, Clark was only one second in front.

Then the announcement came that Surtees had taken the lead a half-lap from the finish. Brabham tried to pass Surtees on the final turn but Surtees led by a car length when they crossed the finish line. Brabham was second and Clark was third, three seconds back, coasting across the line with a dead engine.

During the final three laps, Clark thought he was running out of gasoline because the engine was missing and had finally quit on the homestretch. When the crew examined the fuel tank, they found it still contained three gallons. Their explanation was that the gas had turned to foam for some unexplained reason and couldn't be pumped properly.

Clark had not even won the race, but many experts rated his effort as the finest display of Grand Prix driving ever seen.

"When you did get ahead of Jimmy, you always knew he'd come back at you," Hill said. "He was one fellow you could never shake off easily."

Clark demonstrated the superiority of the Lotus 49 by sweeping the final two races of the season, the U.S. and Mexican Grands Prix. But the points he won were not sufficient to overcome Hulme's lead for the championship. That mysterious foam in the fuel tank may have cost him his third title.

Clark won the South African GP to open the 1968 season. It was his 25th Grand Prix victory, breaking the record of 24 career wins set by Juan Fangio. Then in April 1968 Clark died in the crash of a Lotus Formula 2 car at Hockenheim, Germany.

Clark had carved a special niche of greatness in Grand Prix racing. When any driver turns in a splendid performance, it will always be compared to Jimmy Clark's magnificence at Monza.

Andy, Parnelli
and the Whooshmobiles

The 33 cars in the 1967 Indianapolis 500 roared down the main straightaway into the first turn, in a smooth, orderly start. Fastest qualifier Mario Andretti inched into the lead followed by Dan Gurney, Gordon Johncock, A. J. Foyt and Joe Leonard as the field turned left through the first turn and headed down the short chute to the second turn.

Then Parnelli Jones, who had started on the outside of the second row, jabbed his accelerator with his right foot and pulled out around the other cars. Running high on the track through the second turn, something seldom done at Indy, he swept past the leaders. Coming out of the turn, Parnelli's bright red number 40 racer zipped in front of Andretti into the lead. The turbine revolution had struck the 500!

Jones was driving a turbine-powered car entered by

Parnelli Jones, in the strange off-center turbine car, leads the pack in the 1967 Indianapolis 500.

Andy Granatelli and the STP Corporation, the most controversial machine in the long history of auto racing at the Indianapolis Motor Speedway. From the time the car arrived at the track in early May, it had caused arguments among drivers, mechanics and fans.

From its beginning in 1911, the Indianapolis 500 had been a race for cars with internal combustion engines. The other 32 cars in the 1967 race were powered by turbo-charged Ford and Offenhauser engines, huge, noisy versions of the engine which had made the automobile an important part of modern life. Although the Fords and "Offies" were bigger and more powerful than the engine in a family car, they operated on the same principle—internal combustion.

Now they were faced with Andy Granatelli's "whooshmobile," which made a noise similar to that of a household vacuum cleaner. Granatelli had a history of supporting lost causes. During the previous 20 years, he had tried unsuccessfully to win the 500 both as a driver and car owner. His Novi cars became famous for their failures, and some called Andy "the world's biggest loser." But his new turbine car was something else again. Racing traditionalists were afraid that it would make Granatelli a winner and revolutionize racing.

The idea of adapting a turbine engine for racing had been tried with little success by other teams. But Granatelli was convinced that the engine was ideal, and he devoted the vast resources of his STP team to building a turbine car. He had worked on the unconventional racer for three years.

From the outside, the turbine car looked different

from the long, lean, rear-engined Indy cars. It was wider because the engine was beside the driver. Some detractors claimed the car looked like a big red pancake.

But the engine itself was the real difference. In an internal combustion engine, fuel and air are mixed and ignited in a closed chamber. The force of the explosion drives pistons, which in turn power the car. In a turbine engine, the compressed gases from the ignition of the fuel and air rush past two turbine wheels which resemble multi-bladed propellers, forcing them to turn and providing a direct source of power.

Granatelli's engine was built by Pratt and Whitney, a division of United Aircraft. The same engine was used in wood-chippers in pulp and paper mills, snow blowers, boats and helicopters. Five of the same engines powered the fast turbo-train on the run from Toronto to Montreal.

The Granatelli car had many practical advantages, too. Because of the direct nature of the power supply, the car had no gears to change and no clutch. Its four-wheel drive gave the car great traction and stability. And it burned kerosene, a much less expensive and easier to handle fuel than the sophisticated alcohol-based fuels used by the other cars. Finally, there was none of the ear-splitting noise to wear out a driver.

Still, when Granatelli offered Parnelli Jones a chance to drive the big turbine car, Parnelli was skeptical.

"Sure, I had my doubts," said Jones, who had won the Indy in 1963 and was a big name in U.S. auto racing. "I'd driven internal combustion cars a long time. But I looked at the car and realized it was no freak machine. A lot of money had been spent on its construction, and it was a sanitary car.

"But I didn't know about that ol' jet engine, and I had to be shown. I took a test drive at Indy and did a 162-mile per hour lap right off the bat. There were bugs to iron out of the chassis and handling but I was convinced."

The 550 horsepower from the engine produced a tremendous acceleration boost out of the turns, a force which Jones called "ungodly."

"At first I could hardly believe the acceleration," Jones said. "The thrust of that engine was blinding. When I came out of the corners and stepped on it, sometimes I figured I'd be flying any second. We knew the engine could run forever, but we didn't know if the drive train could stand up to the tremendous thrust of the engine for 500 miles. Also, when you get going that fast that quickly on the straights, you have to slow down for the next turn. We weren't sure if the brakes would stand up to the strain."

Assorted protests were launched against the turbine car by other drivers.

"I've always said Indianapolis was a proving ground for automobiles, not airplanes," Foyt said.

"The turbine should be put in a special class," commented Andretti. "If it isn't, the 500 will become a silent race and the spectacle will be ruined. If it stays in one piece on race day, the rest of us will have a nice little competition for second place."

Andretti earned the pole position at 168.982 miles

The huge turbine engine sits next to the driver, giving the car its lop-sided appearance.

per hour. Jones was sixth on the starting grid at 166.975. Andretti accused Jones of "sand-bagging," running below the car's potential in practice and qualifying.

Jones claimed he was unable to push the car to its limits because he was still learning to drive it. The major problem he encountered was throttle lag, a slight hesitation between the time he depressed the accelerator and the response of the engine.

Race day was cloudy and cool when the 33 cars started. Jones quickly took the lead. Despite running under caution flags for five laps, he built his lead to 19 seconds over Dan Gurney before rain halted the race after 16 laps.

"I figured I could get an early lead, but I didn't think I could do it on the first lap," said Jones while waiting for the skies to clear. "Coming out of the first turn, the other cars stayed low on the track so I just went high around them. I really didn't put my foot down. I can't do that because it's a long race. The power of that engine would tear up the transmission if I gave it full blast over a long period."

Late in the afternoon, the race was postponed until the next day. On the single-file restart, Jones again sped away from the traditional cars. His lead varied from 13 to 55 seconds over Gurney and A. J. Foyt. Gurney was in first place briefly when Jones was forced to the infield grass by a spinning car, but the turbine quickly regained the top spot.

When Gurney was forced out by mechanical problems, Foyt moved into second place, driving steadily but not attempting to chase the front-running machine.

Foyt had said before the race that he was certain the turbine car would not finish. The previous evening he told friends that he should charge the track bank interest "for keeping my first prize money overnight."

"I knew dead certain inside me that the jet car was going to break," Foyt said.

Yet when the race entered its final ten laps, Jones appeared certain of victory. His joyous crew flashed "easy" signs to him on the pit-board. The big car was running flawlessly, well below its top potential, because no other driver was even close. Then, when

Jones was on his 197th lap, only three laps from victory lane, one of sport's most dramatic and heart-breaking events happened.

As Foyt roared down the main straightaway, Parnelli's turbine was three-quarters of a lap ahead of him. The main grandstand crowd swung its eyes from Foyt to turn four to see the turbine. The big red car didn't come around the corner. In the STP pit, Andy Granatelli threw up his hands and the crew started to run towards the corner.

Six dollars worth of ball bearings in the quick-change gear box had failed, and the car was thrown into neutral. The car coasted slowly around the turn and into the pit lane. Jones climbed out, took off his helmet while talking with Granatelli, then sat on the

Sponsor Andy Granatelli and Jones show their disappointment after the car was forced out of the race with three laps to go.

pit wall, head bowed, tears rolling down his cheeks.

Foyt's orange car appeared out of turn four to a thunderous roar from the crowd. He moved down the straight, glanced at the crippled turbine car and waved to his pit crew.

The drama of the day was still not over. When Foyt was on his final lap, he had a premonition of trouble on the main straight. He was correct: Five cars were involved in a spinning, wall-banging crash.

"I don't know why, but I just knew there was going to be a crash there," Foyt said. "I slowed down to 100 miles per hour and when I looked around the fourth turn, there was the mess. I put the car in low gear and pulled down to the inside of the track. I saw a clear lane through the smoke so I stepped on it and got through."

Foyt was greeted in victory lane by his happy crew while the Granatelli team sadly pushed the turbine car back to its garage on Gasoline Alley. The crew disassembled the gear box and placed two small gears and two rings of ball bearings on a towel on a table for reporters to view. Several bearings had flat sides.

"There was no indication that it was coming," said the dejected Jones. "The car just quit all of a sudden as if it had been thrown out of gear. At first I thought I had run out of fuel."

Victory in the 500 denied him once again, Andy Granatelli sat down next to his turbine beauty and cried.

"I'm thinking seriously of getting out of racing," he said. "How can I stand another thing like this? Four stinking laps to go and this had to happen."

The turbine car failed again in the 1968 Indy 500, as driver Joe Pollard clearly indicates.

Granatelli, of course, returned to Indianapolis in 1968 with three turbine-powered cars, driven by Joe Leonard, Graham Hill and Art Pollard. Although rule changes had reduced the engine's power by limiting the size of the air intake, Leonard and Hill were the two fastest qualifiers for the race, sharing the front row with Bobby Unser.

Leonard took the lead on the start, then was passed by Unser on lap eight. On lap 174, Leonard took control when Unser made a pit stop. Once again, the Granatelli turbine appeared on its way to victory.

A crash on lap 181 brought out the yellow flag for ten laps while debris was cleared from the track. On lap 191, Leonard was given the green flag. When he accelerated to regain racing speed, the car slowed suddenly and Leonard pulled off the track near the first turn. The fuel pump drive shaft had snapped when he accelerated. Earlier, Hill had hit the wall with his car, and Pollard's turbine dropped out with the same problem as Leonard's car. History repeated when Bobby Unser drove past the crippled turbine in an internal combustion car to take the victory.

Andy Granatelli had no more chances to test his turbine car at Indianapolis. Further rules changes finally outlawed the turbine altogether. Two unpredictable mechanical failures had made the "jet car" just another chapter in Granatelli's long, unsuccessful quest for victory—but not before the turbines provided two of the most dramatic finishes in Indy history.

9

A Cannon Booms in the Rain

John Cannon was a good auto racer who never attained great success. If he had driven for a factory team in a new car, he might have moved into racing's front ranks. But like many drivers, he had to scratch and scramble to finance his racing effort. He drove older cars on a limited budget, hoping to find the pot of gold at the end of racing's rainbow.

Born and raised in England, Cannon was a pilot in the Royal Air Force and later worked for a cargo airline. In 1957 he migrated to Canada where he became interested in racing. He climbed quickly through the club levels of the sport and appeared to have the talent for big league competition. But racing continued to be a struggle, a constant hunt for sponsors and better cars.

Cannon moved to the United States in 1963 and

drove for several car owners including John Mecom, the Texas millionaire, and the late Dan Blocker, "Hoss Cartwright" of the "Bonanza" television show. But luck just never seemed to ride with Cannon all the way. He often drove poor cars, and when he did get a good one, mechanical problems knocked him out of races. He formed his own racing team, but came to consider it a good season when he broke even.

To an independent driver on a low budget, the Canadian-American Challenge Cup Races (the Can-Am series) represented an enormous attraction. The purses were rich indeed, and a winner of one race could win an average man's yearly income. But the fields were jammed with top international drivers with new cars: Bruce McLaren, Denis Hulme, Jim Hall, Peter Revson, Mark Donohue, Dan Gurney and others.

In 1968, Cannon had a three-year-old McLaren M3-Chevrolet which he had driven with some success in the U.S. Road Racing Championship. When the Can-Am series opened in September, Cannon wanted to enter but didn't have the money to transport his car and mechanics back east from his home base in California. So he missed the first three races of the series. His mechanics, who were friends of Cannon's, were probably relieved. They realized they would be paid only if Cannon earned some prize money.

Then, when the series moved west for the fourth race of the schedule on the Laguna Seca track near Monterey, California, Cannon made his first start. The crew prepared his car as well as their small budget allowed. Young engine-builder Higgs Murphy pieced together a 365-cubic-inch displacement Chevrolet engine from the team's available engine parts. The first question was whether the old rebuilt machine could finish the race. The second question was how far up Cannon could finish anyway against the 427-cubic-inch Ford and Chevy engines in the better cars.

During practice for the Laguna Seca race, Cannon was asked why he continued racing under such discouraging circumstances. "I'm racing because that's the only thing I want to do," he replied. "Sure, it's a struggle, but what comes easy in this world? I think I'm a good race driver, and someday I'll get the chance to prove it."

Cannon pushed the old McLaren to the limit in qualifying for the race. He was 15th on the starting grid, averaging 101.589 miles per hour around the tight 1.9-mile Laguna Seca track. The top qualifier, Bruce McLaren, in his expensive Team McLaren car, was four miles per hour faster.

On the Saturday night before the race, Cannon was approached by a group of California racing enthusiasts who offered to purchase his old McLaren for $7,000 to run in club races. Broke and discouraged, Cannon agreed and sold the car on the spot. But he insisted that he be allowed to complete the Can-Am series in the car. The new owners agreed, and provided that Cannon would keep 40 per cent of any money he won.

Laguna Seca means "dry lagoon." But on race day it rained. One of auto racing's oldest cliches is that "rain is the old equalizer." It was especially true in Can-Am racing because the big cars had so much power in relation to their weight. On a dry track, the

It appears that Bruce McLaren is leading in the 1968 Can-Am race at Laguna Seca. But John Cannon in car 62 (top left) is lapping the field on his way to a great upset victory.

top cars, the McLaren, Donohue, Gurney and Hall machines, were nearly unbeatable. But they needed maximum traction for their power to be transformed into performance.

On a wet track, where traction was poor, the power of the big cars made them difficult to control. The slightest over-acceleration spun the tires and caused the car to slide sideways. Under-powered cars, such as Cannon's and the equally ancient McLaren driven by young Canadian driver George Eaton, had an advantage. Their small engines didn't spin the wheels as easily on the wet track as the big 427 engines.

The track was wet before the race began, and the racing teams began changing tires. The wide, almost treadless "dry" tires would make the cars helpless on a wet track. A thin layer of water would build up between the tire and the track, making the roadway seem as slick as ice. Rain tires had grooves in their tread which prevented the water from building up under the tire's surface, providing much better adhesion to the track.

John Cannon had no rain tires. "I hardly had the money to buy four good dry tires," he said later. He approached Firestone tire expert Bruce Harre to see if any rain rubber were available. The only tires Harre could provide were a set of European Formula 1 rain tires which the other drivers had ignored.

Cannon tried the tires in the short warm-up session just before the race and discovered that they provided maximum adhesion.

"If conditions stay the same, this race is mine," said Cannon when he pulled into his pit after the warm-up.

His lap times in the practice were two to four seconds faster than any other driver's, but few observers even noticed.

Mid-afternoon race time approached, and the rain fell more heavily. The steady downpour forced the 28,000 spectators to seek shelter under trees, umbrellas and bits of plastic sheeting.

The cars formed up in the rain on the starting grid for the 80-lap race. Jim Hall's Chaparral went no further. An engine backfire jammed the starter, and his car was pushed off the track to the pits.

The cars spun their wheels and moved away for the pace lap. Even at low speeds, the drivers found that the wet track was treacherous. The slightest error could cause a spin. In the cockpit of number 62, John Cannon was extremely confident. Unless he accelerated or turned suddenly, his rain tires gave him good road-holding stability.

When the green flag fell, Cannon already was making his charge. At the end of the first lap, he had moved up from 15th to 8th place, driving as surely as if the track were dry. When the field came around to start lap four, the spectators couldn't believe their eyes. Cannon was fifth and challenging leaders McLaren, Hulme, Donohue and Revson. On lap six he passed all four to take the lead. One lap later, he was seven seconds in front of second-place McLaren.

"It was just bloody incredible," said McLaren after the race. "Cannon was driving as if the track was dry. He could go around a whole pack of people in a corner and make it look routine. I couldn't believe it."

Like a sure-footed cat, Cannon continued to build

his lead. By lap 15, he had lapped all the cars up to eighth place. A lap later he had a close call when he passed Gurney going through the hairpin turn near the pits.

"People don't pass there often in the dry," Gurney said. "When I saw Cannon pull alongside my car there, I thought I was seeing things."

The other drivers had problems with their goggles fogging up, but Cannon even had a solution for that. He had cut slits in his goggles which kept them clear. However, some of the water and oil thrown up by the other cars went through the slits and into his eyes, which were sore and swollen for several days after the race.

"Once, when I was passing a slower car, I had to hold one eye open with my fingers because of all the junk that was going through the slits," Cannon said. "But at least my goggles weren't fogging."

While the other drivers had a miserable afternoon, including pit stops for clean goggles, Cannon and his close friend Eaton, who was in his first season of Can-Am racing, had a merry old time.

By lap 35, Cannon had lapped the entire field and was still lengthening his lead. Eaton had moved from an 18th starting position to fourth place.

Cannon later said, "My only problem came because we didn't have very good pit equipment and my crew was having trouble telling me what was going on, how fast I was going and how much of a lead or defecit I had on the cars around me. We just had a blackboard and in the wet, it wasn't very good. Then one lap I came around, there was a real pit board with information on it. I wondered what was going on."

Jim Hall, who had been forced out of the race on the starting grid, had volunteered his magnetic pit board to the Cannon crew. Hall himself took over direction of Cannon's race.

Cannon almost was involved in a five-car tangle in the hairpin turn at one point, but the amazing grip of the Firestone tires permitted him to thread his way through the spinning cars. He maintained his pace at an average speed of 85 miles per hour, an incredible feat on a track made slippery not only by the rain but by the oil thrown from the cars.

At the finish Cannon was one lap plus 5.4 seconds in front of Hulme with young Eaton a strong third. Cannon had also run the fastest single lap in the race, almost four seconds quicker than Hulme's best time.

Cannon's victory was tremendously popular, and he received a long standing ovation from the other drivers at the victory banquet that evening. His first prize money was $19,950. Although he kept only 40 percent of it because of his agreement with the purchasers of the car, he earned enough to pay his bills.

"I'm going to get a tribe of Indians to do a rain dance at every race," a happy Cannon told reporters.

George Eaton offered a delightfully whimsical explanation for the success of the Canadians, he and Cannon, in the rain. "All Canadian drivers are good 'mudders'," he said. "The intense cold of our winters tends to paralyze that portion of our brain that normally tells a person to come in out of the rain. As a result, we dash about in the worst kinds of weather without really knowing any better. It gives us a great

John Cannon celebrates after the race—his first big win.

competitive advantage over better adjusted drivers."

The victory was the big break Cannon had sought throughout his career. In 1969 he was hired by Starr Racing, a top team in the Continental Formula 5000 series. A year later, Cannon won the championship in that series. But whenever Cannon's name is mentioned, racing people first recall his remarkable accomplishment in the rain at Laguna Seca.

10

Moss and Monaco

The 1961 season was a year of transition in Grand Prix racing, and the odds were decidedly against British driving star Stirling Moss.

Many experts claimed Moss was the most talented driver in the history of auto racing, and he was certainly unmatched in versatility. While Juan Manuel Fangio had been even better in Grand Prix cars, Moss won in all types of machine: Formula 1, sports cars, sedans and endurance cars. No driver ever tackled a schedule as demanding as his, and none could equal his overall record. During his career he won more than 40 per cent of his races.

Moss also was a man of enormous determination. In the Belgian Grand Prix at Spa, midway through the 1960 season, a hub carrier on his Lotus broke at 130 miles per hour. The car crashed into a bank and

Stirling Moss, one of racing's greatest competitors.

flipped over. Moss sustained a broken back, fractures of both legs and a broken nose, and there were predictions that his career was finished. However, he made a remarkable recovery and was driving with his oldtime verve less than a year later.

Despite his incredible record of achievement, Moss never won the world driving championship, awarded to the top Grand Prix racer. He finished second four times and was third during three other seasons, but the top prize always eluded him.

A major reason for not winning the world title was Moss' intense nationalism. He would drive only British-owned cars and turned down several lucrative offers from top European teams, including Ferrari. Several of the British teams were private entrants and lacked the vast resources of the big factory teams.

The "underdog" role was one which Moss played extremely well. He seemed to prefer a car which he had to drive to its limits. But in 1961 he faced enormous handicaps. Not only was he coming back from his serious injuries, but the "formula" which governed the construction of Formula 1 cars was changed that year, reducing the maximum piston displacement from 2.5 liters to 1.5 liters.

The British car makers, who had dominated the world championship series in the old 2.5 liter cars, had been bitterly opposed to the revision of the formula because they had no suitable 1.5 liter engine. They knew that to develop a new engine would be costly and time-consuming. In fact, the switch to a smaller engine would probably eliminate them from contention in the 1961 races.

When the 1961 season opened, the Ferrari team of Italy had a clear advantage. Ferrari had perfected a 1.5 liter engine for its Formula 2 cars the previous season. Now the Italian factory put its proven engine into a new Formula 1 car. (Unlike previous Ferraris, the new car was designed with its engine in back—other teams had had rear engines for several years.)

Moss began the season driving a year-old Lotus car for the privately entered team of Rob Walker. While the Ferrari engines produced 190 horsepower, the outdated four-cylinder power plant in Moss' Lotus put out only 150. On courses with long straightaways, the Ferrari drivers—Phil Hill and Richie Ginther of the United States and Wolfgang Von Trips of Germany—would be able to run away from Moss even if his car handled better on the turns.

Even in the Monaco Grand Prix, Moss was the underdog. But the Monaco course was a "driver's course," giving a great driver at least some chance. The race was run through the streets of Monte Carlo (Monaco's only city). The route was 1.9 miles long, featuring tight corners and almost unbelievable hazards. Cars had to race at 100 miles per hour or more through narrow streets past marble buildings and glass storefronts, along the harbor (where the slightest mistake could earn a driver a free bath) and even through a dark tunnel.

The race was the type of challenge which always brought out the best in Moss. Many times during his career he had won in outclassed, underpowered cars. From the time practice and qualifying opened at Monaco in 1961, Moss demonstrated that he intended to deliver his best effort.

On the tight Monaco course, a driver's starting position assumed great importance because passing other cars was extremely difficult. Since the fastest cars in the qualifying laps got the front positions, Moss had to qualify near the top. During qualifying, the Ferraris would run a fast lap, and Moss would push his little Lotus to the limit to top their speed.

His crew had even stripped the side panels from the car to save every possible ounce of weight. Spectators could even glimpse his feet working the brake, clutch and accelerator pedals as he streaked by.

On race day the field formed for the start on the harbor promenade, the blue waters of the Mediterranean seas making this the most beautiful spot in auto racing. Moss sat in pole position as the fastest qualifier in his bright blue Lotus. Richie Ginther in his red Ferrari was beside him and Scotland's Jim Clark, in the second year of what was to become a brilliant career, rounded out the front row in a factory-entered Lotus. Phil Hill and Von Trips in the other Ferraris, and England's Tony Brooks in a BRM were in the second row.

When the flag dropped to start the race, Ginther used his power edge to win the drag race with Moss into the "Gasworks Turn" and take the lead. Clark jumped into second place for one lap. Then his engine failed. That left Moss in second, but Ginther had pushed his Ferrari to a quick six-second lead. The Ferrari team strategy had Ginther running for the lead while Hill and Von Trips stayed slightly off the pace to preserve their cars.

Pushing the Lotus to the absolute limit, Moss slowly reduced Ginther's lead, cutting it by a fraction of a second each lap. The Ferrari moved out a little on the straights but Moss' superior cornering allowed him to close the gap.

On lap ten Moss was on the Ferrari's tailpipe, moving out on the narrow corners as if he intended to pass. Although Ginther pushed his car as hard as he could, he was unable to shake the Lotus.

Four laps later as they approached the hairpin turn,

Moss whizzes past the harbor in the 1961 Monaco Grand Prix.

Moss made one of racing's historic moves. He started to pull alongside the Ferrari in the inside of the track just before the turn, then switched suddenly to the outside line. He was just inches away from hitting the curb, a big danger at Monaco because it could send a car flying into the air. Entering the tight turn, Moss pulled even with the Ferrari, then burst ahead. The large crowd greeted the maneuver with a standing ovation.

Yet the spectators were certain that Moss would be unable to maintain the lead through the 100 laps. One of the three Ferraris would certainly stay close to Moss and pass him sooner or later on a straightaway.

The Ferraris continually nipped at Moss' heels, trying to force a mistake or make the pace so fast that the underpowered Lotus would break under the stress.

Running second, third and fourth were Ferraris driven by Hill, Ginther and Von Trips.

Losing the lead was only one of the dangers Moss faced. The others came from the course itself. "Driving through a corner at the absolute maximum on most courses was one thing," he once said. "There was a stretch of grass beside the track to skid on if you lost control. But when you're flat out in a turn at Monaco and you lose it, you bang a wall. Well, that's something else completely.

"Another problem at Monaco is that the course is sheltered in some spots, especially in the tunnel. The exhaust from the cars doesn't clear away too quickly. It's trouble when you get a few good whiffs of it while following another car closely."

As the race progressed, the Ferrari drivers increased the pace as much as possible, moving up beside Moss whenever they could. Although the pressure on him was incredible, Moss never wavered, never drove the car at anything less than perfection. His only hope of holding the lead was to gain ground on the turns to make up for the ground he lost on the straights.

Entering some of the tighter turns, Moss had to slow the car from 100 to 25 miles per hour in a very short distance. He did it with smoke belching up from the tires as the spectators watched his feet flick from accelerator to the brake through the gaps in the side of his car.

Phil Hill remained in second place until lap 75 when he waved Ginther past him to take up the chase. Ginther was one of the top chargers in Formula 1 racing, a driver who could sustain a brutal pace for long periods. Later, Ginther claimed he had never driven a better race in his life. But his repeated tries to pass the Lotus were turned back by Moss' amazing moves through the turns.

The finish saw Moss 3.6 seconds in front of Ginther. The 80,000 spectators cheered him for several minutes when he took the checkered flag. The opposition crews applauded in a rare tribute as he drove back to his pits. Moss' average speed of 70.71 miles per hour established a record for the race.

The crowds lining the streets of picturesque Monaco cheer as Stirling Moss crosses the finish line.

Later, Moss estimated that he drove to the very limit, absolutely flat out, on at least 90 of the 100 laps. "I had to drive as fast as I could possibly push the car, right to the edge of its limits to stay ahead of the Ferraris," he said. "I never drove in a race in which I was as close to the edge for so long as that one.

"The average person just has no idea how tiring almost three hours of racing like that really is. Even in a normal race, Monaco is a course which requires constant concentration because there's no room to correct an error. But in tight competition like that, concentration was even more intense. You have to change gears maybe 1,500 times in the race plus all the work with your feet. I was physically whipped when that race ended."

Moss continued to drive his old Lotus with his usual virtuosity over the remainder of the season. He won the German Grand Prix at Nurburgring in another great performance, but Phil Hill and Ferrari won the world driving championship.

In April 1962, less than a year after Monaco, Moss suffered critical injuries in a crash at Goodwood, England. He recovered but found out that his unbelievable reflexes had been damaged. He never raced again.

However, years later, after many other drivers had come and gone, Moss was still considered one of the greats of racing. That flawless drive through the streets of Monte Carlo alone was enough to prove the case.

11

Farewell, Roadsters!

In 1961, Jack Brabham entered the Indianapolis 500 with a small rear-engined car built in England by John Cooper. Although Brabham was a champion driver and car builder in Europe's Grand Prix circuit, the American drivers laughed at him and his car. These Americans had battled the two-and-a-half mile Speedway for years in big, front-engined roadsters. The standard Indy cars were heavy and powerful—they boasted 200 more horsepower than Brabham's little Cooper. American drivers and fans were convinced that the huge Offenhauser engines would blast the newcomer off the track—or at least leave it in the dust.

Then Brabham qualified his drastically under-powered car at a speed only two miles per hour slower than the 500 pole-sitter Eddie Sachs. But still the Indy

When Jack Brabham entered this rear-engined Cooper in the 1961 Indy 500, Indy veterans laughed and called it the "funny car."

establishment refused to acknowledge its merits.

"The car was very fragile, nothing but a few pieces of junk held together by chicken wire," said A. J. Foyt, a top American driver. "I was afraid chunks would start to fall off it and be a risk to other drivers."

In the early 1960s world auto racing was divided into two distinctly separate camps. In the United States, power was the main thing for racing on the oval tracks. The European group, which raced mainly on road courses, emphasized the handling and versatility of their cars rather than sheer horsepower. American drivers raced in America, and European drivers in Europe.

The American drivers regarded Grand Prix racing as "sissy" and considered the small rear-engined cars as mere toys compared to the big Indy roadsters. The Grand Prix stars viewed the U.S. drivers as big, hairy-chested brutes who drove their powerful but awkward machines with sheer strength and little skill.

British builder John Cooper had started the swing to rear-engined Grand Prix cars in the late 1950s. Before long, all Formula 1 teams joined the move. By 1961 the engines of all Formula 1 cars were behind the driver. The modern race car had been born.

When the rear-engined cars were successful on the world's most difficult road courses, the builders began to look towards Indianapolis and the huge purse offered in the 500-mile race. Brabham's 1961 trip to Indy in what the American drivers called a "funny car" was only the beginning of a trend that revolutionized the sport. He qualified for the 15th starting position and finished a creditable ninth. To open-minded spectators, Brabham's drive was a success, showing that a lighter, more maneuverable car could hold its own even when it gave up 200 horsepower to the roadsters.

Mickey Thompson of California was one who noticed Brabham's performance. In 1962 he entered three cars with a radical rear-engine design. Dan Gurney, the top American driver in Grand Prix racing, earned a 500 starting berth in one of them, but none of the cars finished near the top.

Now Gurney was convinced that cars based on the design of Formula 1 machines were ideal for Indy. He had brought Colin Chapman, the British designer-builder of the great Lotus cars to Indianapolis for the race. Gurney convinced Chapman that a new rear-engined car should be built for an assault on the 500.

The "funny car" revolution at Indianapolis began in earnest in 1963 when eleven of the 66 cars entered were rear-engined. Mickey Thompson returned with five of them, and Chapman entered three new Lotus 49 models. The Lotus drivers were Gurney and Scotland's Jimmy Clark, the top driver in Grand Prix racing.

Most Indy drivers and builders still laughed at the new rear-engined cars, however. The new Lotus was of single-shell construction with no chassis to match the heavily built roadsters. The car's one-piece body contained the cockpit and long, slender fuel tanks beside the driver and a light tubular frame at both ends of the body.

The Lotus 49 was powered by a 370 horsepower Ford engine based on the power-plant in Ford's Fairlane passenger cars. By contrast, the Offenhauser engines in the roadsters produced 450 horsepower. But the Lotus weighed only 1,100 pounds, compared to the roadsters' 1,450 pounds and up. The Lotus was faster through the corners, its light weight was easy on tires, and the gasoline-burning engines needed one less stop for fuel than the roadsters, which burned an alcohol-based fuel.

The Indy oldtimers didn't like gasoline. "Those funny cars are dangerous because of the gasoline," said one 500 veteran. "If they smack the wall, the impact will explode those tanks, which are right beside the driver."

The new cars were not the only subject of conversation in 1963, however. Driver Jimmy Clark was another. Clark was in the midst of winning his first driving championship in the Grand Prix series. Yet he was an introverted, rather shy young man who didn't enjoy the glare of publicity at Indianapolis. And he was angered when he had to pass the Indy rookie test, although he was an experienced Grand Prix racer.

"They treated the road racers like bloody little kids," Clark complained. "Did they think we couldn't make left-hand turns because we hadn't been here before? There were hundreds of reporters at Indy who were trying to build up a feud between the Grand Prix drivers and the Indy people. What a lot of nonsense! I wasn't there to feud with anyone. I just wanted to drive my car as well as possible."

The top qualifier for the 1963 race was Parnelli Jones, who had been a leader in the 1961 race but had never won. Once again he was driving his famous "Ol' Calhoun" roadster, owned by J. C. Agajanian, the wealthy Californian who operated a large garbage disposal company. ("I'm in the 'used food' business," Agajanian said.)

Indy veterans Jim Hurtubise and Don Branson shared the front row with Parnelli. Clark, who had excited the Indy crowd with his very smooth driving, was in the second row. Gurney had qualified the Lotus team's back-up car well back in the field after he had rammed the wall with his top machine in the qualifying laps.

The 1963 Indy 500 was the most controversial in the

long history of the race. Because he had to make three pit stops for fuel to only two for Clark, Jones was determined to build as large a lead as possible. At the start, Jones quickly moved in front while Clark drove conservatively.

"Those big roadsters used up a great deal of the road which made passing a bit tricky," Clark said. "In the early laps, I merely wanted to stay within sight of the leaders and size up the situation."

An early accident brought out the yellow caution flag under which the drivers are supposed to reduce their speed and maintain their position. However, Jones lengthened his lead under the yellow. Many observers expected the race officials to penalize him but the officials ignored the move.

Clark was in ninth position, just behind Gurney, when the green flag appeared again. As the roadsters in front of them began to make their first pit stops at the 60-lap mark, the Lotus drivers moved up. When Jones stopped on lap 64, Clark and Gurney were in the first two positions.

The Lotus crew was unaccustomed to pit stops and when Gurney made his first halt for fuel, they needed 52 seconds to complete the job. Jones charged past Gurney. Then Clark made a 33-second stop a few laps later, and Jones moved past him, too, taking a 48-second lead. However, Parnelli had two more stops to make, the Lotus cars only one.

Because Jones was a veteran of the 500 and knew all the tricks, he made his pit stops under caution flags and was able to hold his lead. But with 60 laps remaining in the race and Jones 40 seconds in front,

By 1963, rear-engined cars had the inside track. Here Jim Clark (9) passes one of the traditional bulky roadsters.

Clark began to gain. As he weaved through the roadster traffic, the huge crowd began to cheer his driving skill.

Suddenly, black smoke belched from Jones' car. The side-mounted oil tank had cracked, and the oil was flying out on to the back of the machine and the track, creating very slippery conditions. When Jones slowed slightly, Clark quickly cut his lead to four seconds on the treacherous surface.

At one point, the starter had the black flag in his hand to wave Jones off the track because of the danger created by the oil. However, Agajanian convinced chief steward Harlan Fengler that the crack in the tank was horizontal and because the oil level had dropped below the crack, the leaking had stopped. Colin Chapman argued that Jones should be black-flagged. But Fengler ruled that Jones could continue the race, and he won by 33 seconds over Clark.

"When Parnelli started losing oil and I caught him, I didn't want to risk a spin on the oil trying to pass him," Clark said. "I figured he'd be lucky to finish, but I was wrong."

Arguments raged for months about the outcome of the race. Driver Eddie Sachs, who had spun in the oil, complained about it to Jones at a banquet. Jones punched him in the mouth. Many claimed that Jones should have been penalized for increasing his lead under the caution flag and black-flagged off the track for throwing oil. They hinted that Jones was permitted to continue because he represented the old guard at Indianapolis. Others said that Jones merely had taken advantage of a situation by moving ahead on the caution flag, and that Fengler was correct in allowing him to finish.

The 1963 race was a setback for the supporters of the rear-engined cars, but Jim Clark wasn't discouraged. "I sure want to come back again and race these guys because I learned a lot," he said.

The "funny car" revolution continued in 1964 when 24 of 61 entries were rear-engined machines. Even Jones and A. J. Foyt, both roadster veterans, had rear-engined cars. But mechanical difficulties put the new cars out of action and both men started the race in their traditional roadsters. Lotus returned for the second year with new cars featuring a new Ford engine

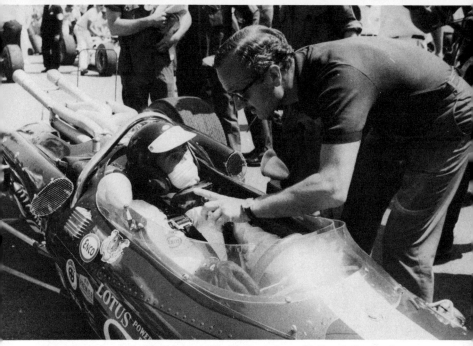

Determined to win in his third try, Jim Clark confers with the designer of his Lotus car, Colin Chapman, before the 1965 race.

which equaled the Offenhauser horsepower. Jim Clark earned the pole position with a record qualifying speed of 158 miles per hour.

The race was a disaster. On the second lap, California sports car driver Dave MacDonald, an Indy rookie in a rear-engined car, lost control in turn four and smacked the wall. The fuel tank split and the car became an inferno. The veteran Sachs rammed Mac-Donald's flaming car and caught fire. Both Sachs and MacDonald died.

When the race was restarted, Bobby Marshman jumped into a 40-second lead over Clark. Then he lost control in a turn and spun to the infield. The damage to his car forced Marshman out of the race and shot

Clark into a big lead, far ahead of Jones and Foyt in their roadsters. But on lap 47, Clark's tires began to shred and he spun off the track. Finally, Jones' car caught fire during a pit stop, and Foyt was handed an easy 500 victory.

Although the rear-engined cars had not yet won a race, they had made their point. In 1965, 44 of 68 entries were "funny cars." Now even the Indy veterans knew that they had to join the revolution if they wished to remain competitive. To many of them, the new machines were a puzzle. Several American drivers complained that the rear-engined cars were much more difficult to drive than their old machines. During the May practice and qualifying periods, there were assorted spins and breakdowns as the old guard attempted to master the new cars.

But no one could halt Clark and his Lotus. Chapman had hired the famous Woods brothers crew from southern stock car racing to man the Lotus pits. Clark qualified his Lotus at 160 miles per hour but lost the pole position to Foyt.

Clark took the lead at the start, then allowed Foyt to move past him for a few laps. The Flying Scot quickly regained the lead and turned the race into a romp, leading on 190 of 200 laps. He finished two minutes ahead of Jones and set a new speed record, averaging nearly 151 miles per hour.

The rear-engine revolution was complete. From then on, the cumbersome front-engined roadster which had made so much racing history at Indianapolis was finished. And the drivers who had laughed at Jack Brabham were driving cars just like his.

12

The Gentlemanly Tiger

Away from the late model stock cars which had carried him to the front rank of drivers on the National Association for Stock Car Auto Racing (NASCAR) Grand National circuit, Bobby Allison was a quiet gentleman.

He was deeply religious, actively involved in civic affairs in his hometown of Hueytown, Alabama, and a devoted father to his four children. He was also popular with the newsmen because he granted interviews and was frank in answering all questions. Allison listed his hobbies as football games, hunting, fishing and playing with his children.

But behind the wheel of his stocker, Allison was a different story. The quiet gentleman off the track was a very aggressive driver, a charger who wanted only to run at the front of the pack. Allison frequently was involved in controversial fender-bashing duels with the other top NASCAR stars and became a part of some of racing's most famous battles.

"Bobby makes a complete personality switch as soon as he fastens his safety harness," said a NASCAR rival. "Out of the car, he's about the quietest, most easy-going guy in the world. In the car he's a tiger who will challenge anyone. He's also a great race driver, one of the best, and certainly the most determined."

Born in Miami, Florida, Allison saw his first auto race at a local stock car track when he was nine, and that day decided he would be a race driver. He had his driver's license at 14 and entered his first race as a high school senior. He opened a garage in Florida where he became a master mechanic, racing under an assumed name in his spare time because his parents strongly objected to the dangerous sport.

Allison was driving modified stock cars, and he soon moved to Hueytown, a suburb of Birmingham, Alabama, which was near several modified tracks. A few years later, his brother Donnie, who also became a top NASCAR star, moved to Hueytown, too.

In the bash-and-crash world of modified stock car racing, only the drivers who fought for every inch of track won many races. Allison quickly showed that he wouldn't be pushed around. Any driver who tried to shove him off the track discovered that he was tangling with a tiger. And when the spectators noticed that the young Allison always seemed to be in the center of the action, he became a big crowd favorite.

Once, Allison figured his car was being used as a battering ram by another driver. When the race ended, he punched his rival, who outweighed him by 50 pounds.

In a famous incident early in his career, Allison encountered four drivers at the Huntsville, Alabama, track who had formed a "team" to prevent his winning the races. In a preliminary heat, the four drivers bumped and blocked him, and one squeezed Allison into the retaining wall. Allison started late in the feature race because of the time needed to repair his car. Then he quickly wiped out the team, bumping two into the wall and one into the infield. They didn't bother him again.

Bobby ran four Grand National races in 1961, but he didn't become a regular on the major league NASCAR circuit until 1965. He had only occasional success until 1970. That year he earned 30 top-five finishes in 46 races, had three wins and collected $130,000 in prize money.

By then, he had confirmed his reputation as a driver who never backed away from an on-track battle. Early in his Grand National career, Allison had begun a battle with Curtis Turner, a folk hero of American racing. Turner was a hard-driving, high-living man who was a big NASCAR winner in the 1950s and 1960s.

Turner had a fighting reputation of his own, and if a young racer could stand up to Turner, he could stand up to anyone. In a 1966 Grand National race at Winston-Salem, North Carolina, the Allison-Turner feud came to a head. Bobby was driving a Chevelle which he had built himself. Running behind Allison, the veteran Turner began to bump his car from the

Bobby Allison (left) roars past a car whose engine has just blown in the 1973 Pennsylvania 500.

rear. Allison allowed Turner to pass, moved up close and to the crowd's surprise, bumped Turner's car solidly a few times. The spectators were amazed that a young driver, in his first full season of Grand National racing, would challenge the wily old Turner.

Turner decided to teach the youngster a lesson. He moved up beside Allison, bashed him and spun the Chevelle. As Turner said later, "The kid was either a slow learner, or a very fast one, I don't know which," because Allison returned the compliment, and Turner was spun out.

Now Turner decided he'd had enough nonsense from the upstart rookie. He waited for the proper moment and slammed Allison broadside to the infield.

Allison came to rest on the infield with a dead engine.
The spectators and Turner figured the battle was over.
But when Turner came around again, Allison's "dead"
engine roared to life, and he slammed broadside into
Turner. That collision put both cars out of the race,
but Bobby Allison's reputation was established beyond
doubt.

"It wasn't my style to start a race with ideas of
hitting another car," Allison said. "But when Curtis
started biffing me, I felt I had to hit him back."

Allison scratched a living on the Grand National
circuit for several years, driving the cars he prepared
himself in the garage behind his Hueytown home. But
an independent racer faced an almost impossible
challenge competing against the factory teams and top
drivers. Following Allison's strong 1970 showing, he
encountered problems in 1971. Halfway through the
season, he was broke and discouraged when his big
break came. He was offered the chance to drive a Ford
for the famous Holman-Moody team, which had split
with its top driver David Pearson. Allison wound up
with eight races and $236,295 in prize money for the
season.

Acquisition of the excellent ride placed Allison in
the front ranks on the Grand National circuit. First
place in the rich super-oval races was hotly contested,
and challenging for it brought Allison into direct
conflict with the cream of the NASCAR drivers,
especially the undisputed king of the high banks,
Richard Petty. Soon the biggest discussion in the stock
car world became the Allison-Petty battle for suprem-
acy.

The roots of the Allison-Petty battle had been planted in 1967. Petty dominated that season in unparalleled fashion, winning 27 of 48 races and a record $130,000 in prize money. Allison was the only other driver who often found the victory circle, winning six races. Their first serious clash came in an unimportant 250-mile race at Weaverville, North Carolina.

Allison had led approximately 400 of the 500 laps on the half-mile track when an accident forced a restart. Allison was caught behind a slow car as the cars took off, and Petty took the lead. When Petty slowed for a corner, Allison bumped him from behind. They bumped all the way down the straightaway. Finally Allison moved around Petty on the inside and went on to win.

"People say that's where the so-called feud between Petty and I started," Allison recalled. "But I didn't bump him deliberately. He slowed down much more quickly than I anticipated, and I couldn't avoid him."

When Allison moved into the very fast Holman-Moody Ford in 1971, he was able to challenge the Petty Plymouth for the lead in many races. The racing press tried to make it a family feud because both drivers' teams contained several relatives. Petty's father Lee, a former great NASCAR driver, was team manager; brother Maurice was the team's engine builder; and a cousin, Dale Inman, was crew chief on Richard's car. Allison's brother Donnie was a regular NASCAR competitor and a member of his brother's crew any time he wasn't racing himself; and Eddie Allison was a mechanic on his brother's car.

When Petty won the Dixie 500 at Atlanta International Speedway to become the first driver to pass the $1,000,000 mark in career winnings, he and Allison had a devastating, fender-bending duel during the final laps.

However, another 1971 race—the 500-mile event at Talladega, Alabama—became a NASCAR legend and will be discussed as long as there is stock car racing. Talladega was slightly different from the other super-ovals. Its 2.66-mile track was arranged in a tri-oval with four high banked corners, an exceedingly fast and tricky challenge for the drivers.

The race had been run at a killing pace, but entering the final lap, three cars were separated by only a few feet. The drivers were Petty, Allison and Pete Hamilton, a young New Englander who had blazed to the top of Grand National racing.

Speeding into the first turn, Allison's Mercury led the Plymouths of Petty and Hamilton. Petty was high on the outside with Hamilton tucked in behind Allison as they jetted down the second straight in a close-quarters triangle of autos.

The 80,000 spectators were on their feet but strangely silent as the three cars sped through turn three and down the short straight to the fourth turn. A small puff of smoke suddenly emerged from the corner. Hamilton's Plymouth went out of control, clipped the wall and spun down the banked track to the bottom, smoke belching from the skidding tires. Petty's car wobbled and came close to spinning out before he fought it under control. Allison came out of the turn low on the track and sped on to take the checkered flag as the victor.

At the post-race press conference, Petty acknowl-

After a big win, Allison clowns with the victory cup.

edged that there had been a battle. Petty claimed Allison had moved in front of him, he had cut hard to the inside, and his car slid sideways into Hamilton's car.

"There's red paint from Allison's car on my car which tells the story," Petty said.

"There's 'Petty blue' paint on my car, too," Allison replied. "There's no reason why Petty had to follow me because the track is four lanes wide. It's not the first time, either. We ran a 200-miler earlier this season and the only part of my car that wasn't dented was the front bumper."

The off-track battle continued verbally for a few days, but then both sides backed down, denying that there was any "bad blood" between them.

"It just seems that in most races Bobby Allison and me wound up fighting for the same spot, first place," Petty said. "Now when a couple of fellas are doing that and want the same piece of track, it can lead to a little trouble."

"The way I look at it, it's mighty nice to be in a position to bash the odd fender with Richard Petty," Allison said. "After all, he's the king."

After all, Allison was a gentleman off the track. But race fans knew that the next time he and Petty scrambled for first place, Bobby would be a tiger, feud or no feud.

13

The Mastery of Stewart

In 1969 Jackie Stewart of Scotland breezed to the world driving championship in a French-built Matra. The car was powered by a Cosworth-Ford engine and prepared by a team led by Ken Tyrrell, the veteran British racing owner and team manager.

Then in 1970 the Matra factory refused to allow Tyrrell to purchase its cars for Stewart. Tyrrell talked with several other car builders, and they too were reluctant to sell their cars for the best driver in Formula 1 racing to handle. If Stewart wanted to drive their cars, they reasoned, why didn't he leave Tyrrell and race for their factory team? He had had several offers, but had decided to stay with Tyrrell.

Finally, Tyrrell purchased a March, the product of a newly formed construction team. But early in the 1970 season the March cars had proved unreliable.

Now Tyrrell decided to build a car himself. Working with designer Derek Gardner, the Tyrrell crew began construction of the car in May 1970 in a garage in one corner of a lumber yard just outside of London. The development of the new car was the best-kept secret in the history of the sport.

"At first, only Gardner, Tyrrell and myself knew about the car," Stewart said. "Then, of course, the crew had to be told when they started to build it. But we wanted the project to be absolutely secret. We figured it would be demoralizing on the opposition to spring a new car on them suddenly. If we had something really good, then it would take them time to catch up. It was a bit of a laugh, really. In a timber yard with a pot-holed road running through it, a car to challenge for the world championship was being built."

Jackie Stewart had begun his racing career in sports car and sedan events in Scotland and England. Then in 1964, Tyrrell had hired the young Scot to drive Tyrrell's Cooper in Formula 3 racing. The Tyrrell team dominated the Formula 3 series in 1964, and Stewart received several offers to drive Formula 1 cars on the Grand Prix circuit.

He joined BRM, a major British car manufacturer, for the 1965 season and scored his first victory in the Italian GP at Monza. He also entered the Indianapolis 500 and had a wide lead when his car lost its oil pressure and was forced out of the race ten laps from the finish.

Stewart spent two more frustrating seasons with BRM and had little success in unreliable cars. Then in

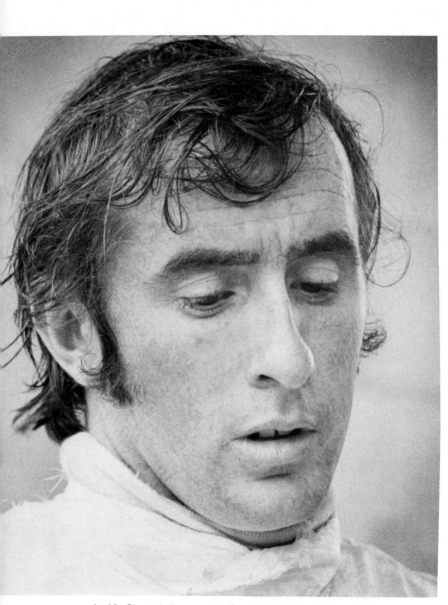

Jackie Stewart, the greatest Grand Prix driver of recent times.

1968, Tyrrell decided to campaign the Matra-Fords. Stewart quickly accepted his offer to drive the Ford-powered cars. The good Tyrrell crew quickly solved the car's problems, and Stewart victories in the Dutch, German and United States races propelled him into contention for the world driving championship. But he lost the crown to Graham Hill in the final race of the season.

In 1969 the Tyrrell-Stewart-Matra combination romped to the world title. Jackie won six of eleven Grand Prix races and became a major celebrity. A quick-witted man, he used his personality and great driving skill to bring in a large annual income. He endorsed a variety of products, was a regular guest on television talk shows and became a familiar spokesman for racing drivers.

With the new March car in 1970, Stewart ran into problems. Lacking a reliable car, he lost his world title to the late Jochen Rindt. Late in the season Stewart and Tyrrell sprang their big surprise on the other Formula 1 teams. The new Tyrrell car made its debut in the final three races of the season. But even the surprise didn't redeem a miserable season. The car showed great potential, but Stewart was forced out of all three events with mechanical problems.

A new Tyrrell chassis was built for 1971, and in the first race of the season, the South African Grand Prix, Stewart finished second. The second race was the Spanish Grand Prix on the Circuito de Montjuich at Barcelona. Stewart was acknowledged as the greatest driver on the circuit, yet he was coming off a bad season, and the new Tyrrell had not yet proved itself.

"I feel we've made good progress with the Tyrrell cars," Stewart said before the race in Spain. "But don't forget that it's still basically a new car. I'm certain we have the correct design. All it needs are some small refinements."

But Jackie couldn't use the car as an excuse forever. Racing fans were wondering what was wrong with *him*. Jackie needed a victory—and the sooner the better.

The Barcelona track was a true road circuit which ran through a park close to the center of the city. On the insistence of the Grand Prix Drivers' Association safety committee, which Stewart headed for several years, heavy steel barriers had been installed along both sides of the track to protect the drivers if they went off the track and the 100,000 spectators who attended the race. The course was 2.35 miles long and included a fast downhill section and several curves which would be negotiated at high speeds.

"It's a track where there's little room for driver error or you'll smack the rails," Stewart commented. "There are very few spots on it where it's easy to pass another car. If you want to win that race, a good grid position is important."

His main opposition was supplied by the Italian Ferrari team with drivers Jackie Ickx, Clay Regazzoni and Mario Andretti. Andretti had finished first ahead of Stewart in the South African race. The Ferrari cars were powered by V-12 engines which gave them a power edge on the Tyrrell and other cars which used the Cosworth-Ford V-8 plants.

The BRM team had two strong drivers in Pedro Rodriguez and Jo Siffert. Stewart's teammate, Francois Cevert, was driving a second Tyrrell. Chris Amon and Jean-Pierre Beltoise drove Matras, the veteran Denis Hulme was racing a McLaren, and rising young stars Ronnie Peterson and Emerson Fittipaldi were driving a March and a Lotus respectively. It was a strong field—nearly every driver was a threat.

The closeness of the 1971 Grand Prix competition was demonstrated in the qualifying laps. Jackie Ickx had the fastest time, and Stewart was only three-tenths of a second slower—yet he started in fourth position. Regazzoni and Amon shared the front row with Ickx, while Rodriguez was beside Stewart in the second row.

At the start of the 75-lap race, Ickx shot ahead of the field. At the end of the first lap, he had a two-second lead on Stewart, who was followed closely by Regazzoni, Amon, Rodriguez and Beltoise. Stewart quickly cut down Ickx's lead and passed the Ferrari on lap six.

Pushing the Tyrrell hard through the tight corners, Stewart slowly but consistently built his margin on Ickx. By lap 20, he was 3.5 seconds in front. Ickx decided to abandon the chase for a few laps to concentrate on saving his car. On lap 43, Stewart's lead was nine seconds.

From the time Ickx joined the Grand Prix circuit in 1968, his detractors claimed that he lacked the consistency of a championship Formula 1 driver. But now, after running a relatively relaxed pace for 20 laps, Ickx suddenly took up the chase. On one lap he chopped 1.3 seconds off Stewart's lead. By lap 60, Ickx had reduced the margin to 4.7 seconds. The huge Spanish crowd, which stood a few feet behind the guardrails along the track, cheered him on.

Stewart makes last-minute preparations for a race.

Then disaster nearly struck the Tyrrell team. When Stewart came up to lap his teammate Cevert, the young French driver moved over. But as Stewart began to pass, Cevert suddenly cut him off. Stewart was forced to slide his car sideways to avoid a collision. Only his great driving skill prevented his hitting either Cevert or the rail.

Ickx was only 3.9 seconds behind Stewart after lap 66. Then he ran the fastest lap of the race, almost a second quicker than his qualifying speed, reducing Stewart's lead to a mere 1.7 seconds.

One of the marks of a great champion is his ability to respond when challenged. When his crew told him on the pit board that Ickx was closing fast, Stewart whipped the Tyrrell around the course for his fastest lap of the race and boosted his lead to more than two seconds again.

Just when the crowd anticipated a wheel-to-wheel feud between the two superb drivers, Ickx went too fast into a hairpin turn and slipped into a sideways skid, losing a precious second to Stewart. At the finish, Stewart was three seconds in front of the Ickx Ferrari. The Tyrrell car had won its first Grand Prix victory.

"The win was especially satisfying to me for two reasons," Stewart said. "First, I was especially pleased to win it for Ken Tyrrell, who took a big gamble in building his own car. Such an effort is a major project for a well-equipped and staffed factory team, but it's a remarkable achievement for an independent entrant. It really was only the fifth race for the Tyrrell car, but it ran perfectly.

"For another thing, I think that Spanish Grand Prix

Stewart takes a tight corner in the 1969 Spanish Grand Prix.

was the toughest, most strenuous and taxing race I'd ever driven. That course seemed ideally suited to the 12-cylinder Ferraris which had a bit of a power edge over my car. I had to drive ten-tenths all the way, leaving very little in reserve—in fact, almost nothing."

Stewart was asked if he could have moved a little more quickly had Ickx closed the gap on him.

"Maybe, but I was running near the limit all the way," he said. "If I had tried to go any faster, I would have risked hitting a barrier. But I doubt if the Ferrari could have passed me. We were both going almost flat out and making use of all the road. It would have been very difficult for either of us to pass."

The victory in Spain launched a remarkable Stewart streak—five triumphs in six races—sweeping him to his second world driving championship. He followed the Spain win with victories in Monaco, France, Great Britain and Germany to clinch the title with four races remaining in the series.

His victory late in the season at the Canadian GP was Stewart's sixth of the season. That was one less than the record of seven wins in one year, established in 1963 by Stewart's close friend, the late Jimmy Clark. In the final race of the season, the U.S. Grand Prix, Stewart was leading when a broken suspension forced him to slow down. He finished fifth.

In 1972 Stewart lost the world driving championship to Emerson Fittipaldi. But then in 1973 he clinched the title even before the last race. At the U.S. Grand Prix in Watkins Glen, Stewart was scheduled to complete the 1973 season, running in his 100th Grand Prix race. But during the trials his good friend Francois Cevert was killed in an accident. Stewart dropped out of the race, and a few days later he announced his retirement. He was sure to be remembered as one of the great drivers in racing history.

Fast and Steady

In 1971 Team McLaren brought another innovation
to Indianapolis. In the past decade, rear-engined cars
based on Grand Prix models had replaced the traditional roadsters. Then for a few years the turbine cars
of Andy Granatelli had threatened a revolution. They
were finally outlawed.

Now, in 1971, the cars pioneered by the late Bruce
McLaren were bringing greater speed to the Speedway. With their wedge shape, they resembled huge
doorstops. And they were equipped with aerodynamic
"wings" on the front and back. Unlike the wings on an
airplane, these were designed to keep the cars on the
ground. They were tilted so that the air rushing by
provided a down-thrust, pushing the car against the
track and giving better traction.

In qualifying for the 1971 Indy, Peter Revson, driving a Team McLaren car, had earned the pole position with a four-lap average speed of 178.696 miles per hour. That smashed the record set in 1968 by Joe Leonard in a turbine car by more than seven miles per hour. Such a jump was considered a rare feat. But experienced observers knew that the McLaren cars were only beginning to realize their potential. Wait until '72, they said.

In November 1971 Bobby Unser turned in laps of 196 miles per hour in a test at the Ontario Motor Speedway in California, a track which was almost identical to Indianapolis. He was driving the Eagle, built by All-American Racers, a car that took advantage of many of the McLaren cars' innovations. Then in March 1972 in a tire-testing session Unser topped 190 miles per hour at Indy itself.

So when practice opened on May 1 for the 1972 Indy, all signs pointed to the fastest times in the history of the "old Brickyard." Before the first weekend of official qualifying, 23 drivers had topped 180 miles per hour and four of them—Bobby Unser, Revson, Gary Bettenhausen and Mike Mosley—were above the 190 mark.

The official qualifying periods were delayed several times because of rain. But when the track dried, the drivers made an amazing assault on Revson's 1971 record. When it was over, Bobby Unser led the way with a four-lap average speed of 195.937 miles per hour, more than 17 miles per hour faster than Revson's '71 time. Never in the history of the Indianapolis track had the qualifying record been increased so steeply.

Revson was second at 192.885 and Mark Donohue was third at 191.408. The 33 cars in the starting field averaged 183.6 miles per hour.

During the week before the race, the experts debated which driver should be called the favorite. Bobby Unser had won the race in 1968 and his Eagle was a great car, so he received much support. Peter Revson had driven a strong second in the 1971 race and was favored by many. The most difficult of the three top drivers to evaluate was Mark Donohue.

Donohue drove for the team headed by Roger Penske, a top road racing driver who had retired to manage. Penske was one of the shrewdest men in the business and Donohue himself had a degree in mechanical engineering. They seemed to make the perfect team—Donohue had been a big winner in sports car, sedan and stock car racing.

But the Donohue-Penske team had been unlucky at Indy. In 1969 Donohue qualified fourth and was running in third after 172 laps when ignition problems forced an eleven-minute pit stop. He still finished seventh and was named rookie of the year. In 1970 he drove a great race but finished second to Al Unser. The next year, after qualifying second, he led the race for 50 laps. Then on lap 66 his transmission failed and he had to drop out.

The Penske team really fell on hard times during practice and qualifying trials in 1972. Although Donohue ended by qualifying third, he had blown out five engines—each of them worth more than $25,000—before succeeding. The crew was exhausted from several all-night sessions installing new engines.

Mark Donohue gets set to drive in the 1969 Indianapolis 500.

As the 1972 race begins, three-time winner A. J. Foyt pulls onto the track late. His car wouldn't start.

The engines that had blown out all had a large turbo-charger, a device that uses the engine's exhaust to produce a power boost. For the race, Donohue had an engine with a smaller turbo-charger. It would put him at a disadvantage on the long straights, but the Penske team hoped that the engine would be more reliable—and less likely to destroy itself.

Still, how were the racing experts to evaluate Donohue? On the one hand, he was a top driver and he had qualified with the third fastest time. On the other hand, he had never been successful at Indy and in practice he had gone through engines faster than other drivers went through fuel. The experts would just have to wait and see.

Race day was bright and sunny. More than 300,000 spectators jammed into the Speedway. But the race itself started in confusion. Speedway president Tony Hulman called, "Gentlemen, start your engines." Thirty-two engines roared to life, but that of A. J. Foyt, who was seeking his fourth 500 victory, did not. The other cars moved away for the parade lap behind the pace car while Foyt's machine was pushed to the end of the pit lane. Following the pace lap, the pace car pulled into the pit lane. Because the cars were not lined up properly, the starter had his hand in the air to signal one more lap. But as the front row approached the starting line, the starter suddenly dropped the green flag.

"We all put up our hands because the yellow caution lights, not the green, were on around the track," Donohue said. "I wasn't in the right gear to go to racing speeds and neither was Revson. When the flag dropped unexpectedly, Bobby Unser just jumped away to a big lead."

Unser quickly opened a sizeable lead and held it for 30 laps. Then the malfunction of a small, obscure part, the distributor rotor, chopped down his Eagle. The first favorite was out of the race.

Gary Bettenhausen, Donohue's teammate, took over first place until lap 53. Then hard-charging Mike Mosley took the lead, but four laps later, the right front wheel flew off Mosley's car on the main straight. The car hit the wall twice and burst into flames. Mosley jumped out, his driving suit aflame. Despite quick action by the firefighters, he suffered severe burns to his hands and feet.

Bettenhausen managed to get past Mosley's spinning car to regain the lead. This time he held it for 102 laps with a smooth, controlled drive. Jerry Grant, driving the Mystery Eagle (so-called because it lacked a sponsor), had charged from his starting position on the fifth row to pass Donohue and take over second place. But the race was three-quarters over, and Bettenhausen appeared to have a big Indy victory in his grasp.

Then the yellow caution flag slowed the field for three laps while debris was cleared off the track. The drivers maintained their positions. But when the green lights came on, Bettenhausen's engine failed to respond when he stepped on the accelerator. The spark plugs had fouled at the slow speeds. Grant and Donohue, running close together, sped by Bettenhausen and into first and second place. Now it seemed to be a simple two-man race.

Then confusion struck again. Grant's crew quickly flashed him a "cool it" sign on the pit board because they believed he was one lap and several seconds ahead of Donohue. The public address announcer agreed briefly. But Donohue's board told him he was only two seconds behind Grant. The announcer then changed his mind and agreed with Donohue's crew. The Grant crew quickly took down the "cool it" sign and frantically flashed the "go" signal to their driver.

Donohue tried to make up the gap on Grant but his smaller turbo-charger wouldn't let him. Grant held his slight margin. Then on lap 188, the situation changed suddenly. Grant made a surprise pit stop. His front left tire had been damaged by a piece of metal on the track. Grant over-shot his own pit and pulled into the

With only twelve laps to go, Jerry Grant pulls into the pit, pointing frantically at his front right tire.

Winner Mark Donohue raises his fist as a salute to the crowd during his victory lap after the race.

pit of his teammate Unser. The crew quickly replaced the tire and added fuel to Grant's car—from Unser's pit tank.

By the time Grant roared back to the track, Donohue was in the lead for the first time in the race. He continued on to the victory and apparently won. But all was not settled yet.

Dan Gurney, manager of the Eagle team, protested

the scoring of the race. He claimed that Grant had run an extra lap and had been ahead of Donohue at the finish. A check of the official scoring tapes confirmed Donohue's victory and the protest was disallowed.

Then the crew of third-place Al Unser lodged a protest against Grant, claiming he had used fuel from another driver's supply. The protest was upheld, and Grant was pushed back to 12th place based on the 188 laps he had completed at the time of the stop. Grant lost $72,000 in prize money for a few gallons of fuel from the wrong tank.

Despite the confusion and the protests, Donohue and the Penske team celebrated their biggest victory. "Maybe my win wasn't overly impressive because I didn't lead every lap and run stronger and faster than everyone else," said Donohue with typical honesty. "I guess the secret here is to be running at the finish. We gambled with a small turbo-charger and it paid off. The Penske team aims at finishing races. We've had some success with that approach."

Page numbers in italics refer to photographs.

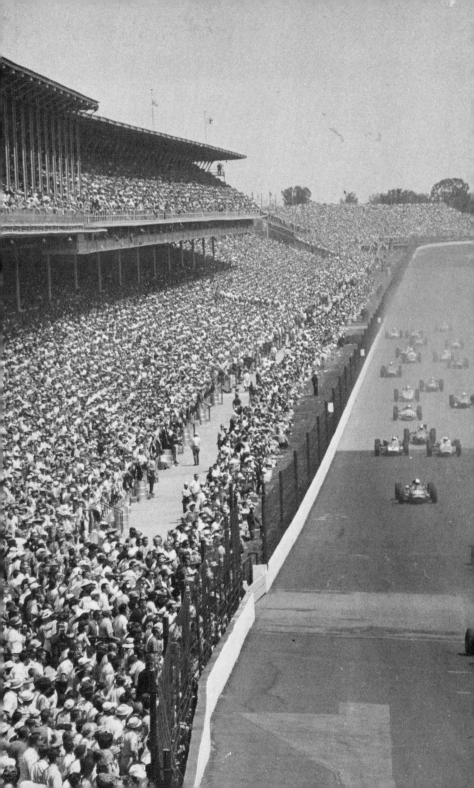